# DIRECTORS' THEATRE

JUDITH COOK

*With a Foreword by JUDI DENCH*

HARRAP    LONDON

TO PHILIP HEDLEY

First published in Great Britain 1974
by GEORGE G. HARRAP & CO. LTD
182—184 High Holborn, London WC1V 7AX

ISBN 0 245 52528 9 (boards)
ISBN 0 245 52564 5 (limp)

*c c*

Composed in IBM Baskerville type by Lonsdale Technical
Printed and bound in Great Britain by REDWOOD BURN
LIMITED Trowbridge & Esher

# Foreword

It is impossible to say what makes an ideal director. The relationship between actor and director is a very personal one — a director that one particular actor finds marvellous to work with may be extremely difficult for another.

I personally feel very much under the thumb of a director, needing his guidance, and find it essential to build up a working relationship with him as he must with the actors. From the director's side, of course, this is particularly difficult: he has to work with, and adapt to, many different people in a wide variety of ways. Directing is such a delicate job, and all the more remarkable since the director must be able to get a production successfully off the ground using a cast he has possibly only just met. Much time has to be spent getting to know how each individual works and appreciating the interaction of the cast as a whole. This book shows quite clearly that there are as many working methods as there are directors. It also shows that an actor is always learning.

The first director I worked with was Michael Benthall at the Old Vic and — as often happens working with directors — he taught me something I hadn't learned at drama school. He explained to me the meaning of the term 'legato' — using words not in a staccato fashion but making them smooth and more drawn out. A small point, but one which has proved a very valuable lesson that has had a lasting effect on my work.

It is important for me — especially with difficult, tense, dramatic pieces — to have a director who approaches his work in an intense but lighthearted way. By initially relaxing and letting off steam the actor can then get down to being completely serious. The borderline between a play that is melodramatic like *The Duchess of Malfi* and one that is meant to be comic is very narrow. I worked with Clifford Williams on *The Duchess of Malfi* and his approach was perfect because he has exactly this ability to be light-hearted while at the same time covering immense ground.

Comedy is notoriously difficult to play. There's always a stage where the play's going well, then another when the laughs are falling flat and it is impossible to tell why. Ronnie Eyre saw me during one of those bad patches in his production of *London Assurance* and helped me enormously when he said: 'Just remember to tell the story — the reality is in telling the story because otherwise you're just doing things for their own sake and not for the sake of telling the story.' It is vitally important to remember this because something 'funny' which has no relevance to the story of the play cannot convey the basic truths involved.

I must say that it is almost impossible to work with a director towards whom the actor has total antipathy — there is no understanding, no *rapport* and no communication. Happily this is the exception rather than the rule! Some directors, like Michael Langham, make the actors feel straight away that they are capable of doing their part, and then give them hell throughout rehearsals. But because the director has already gained the actors' confidence it is an enjoyable and challenging experience.

One of the most exciting directors I have ever worked with is Trevor Nunn. On *The Winter's Tale* I believed entirely in what he was trying to do and we succeeded in many ways in making that difficult story credible. Although he worked incredibly hard on the play it did not *feel* like hard work and he managed to get the very best out of his actors. If I thought I could play a certain piece six different ways he would convince me that I could do it a hundred ways — I felt like a bottomless well. It is a constant and stimulating challenge to have to try and convey words in a multiplicity of ways and it makes actors draw on resources they never knew they had. Help is there if they need it but they can experiment — being watched but not interrupted — until they feel they've got the piece right. It's a wonderful way to work, very fulfilling and productive though it requires a long rehearsal period.

Of course the director's job doesn't end with the final dress rehearsal or public preview. It's no use pretending that there still isn't a lot to be tidied up on the first night and I think the director who not only gives last-minute 'notes' to his actors but also comments while they are actually making up and getting into costume is a great help in calming the nerves — thus getting the best possible performance from the cast.

Theatre audiences today are becoming more and more aware of the director. The point has now been reached when productions are described, for instance, as 'Brook's *Dream*', 'Zeffirelli's *Romeo and Juliet*' etc., and the name of the director becomes just as important as that of the leading actor: in some cases audiences don't even know who's in the cast.

Nor do today's audiences feel it spoils their illusions to know what happens behind the scenes: they want to read how it's done. This book reveals some fascinating aspects and I, personally, feel that it shows that although an actor's job is a hard one, the director's task is much, much harder.

# Preface

When the idea of this book was first suggested it seemed a reasonably easy task. All that was needed was for me to gather up the various profile interviews I had written on directors, and that would be that. As it turned out, I was quite wrong. Virtually every interview was pegged to a single production, and while some of the pieces gave a fairly comprehensive picture of what that person then thought about a production, much essential information was missing. For instance, the original interviews gave no idea why that person had been drawn into directing, rather than acting, banking or even bricklaying. Discussions on individual productions date very quickly too between the time when the writer starts putting them on paper and the time when the book arrives in the shops.

So, as I have always been fascinated by the art of direction, the craft that builds up a production of a play, brick by brick, I went back to those I had interviewed before, but with a different set of questions. This time I wanted to know why they chose to direct, and how they arrived at actually doing it. Then I wanted to know how they work, using some of their productions as a guideline to their working methods. I also wanted to get across something of the way the person thinks and speaks, so to do that I have as far as possible used their own words. Otherwise I might just as well have embarked on a long and boring series of essays which would have read like one rather dreary, overlong newspaper feature.

Just what qualifications are needed to write about the theatre, I do not know. I reviewed for three years, and came into that occupation by chance. Idly standing by the subs' desk in the newspaper office in which I worked, I noticed that the most glamorous of the group was on the telephone. Motioning to me, she said, 'X wants to know if you could review a play for him tonight.' X was the arts editor on a quality paper, not my own, and the whole idea seemed absurd, and anyway fraught with hazard. 'No,' I replied. She went back to the phone. 'He'll pay you thirty pounds,' she hissed. To which the only reply was, 'What time does it start?' and so I became a theatre critic. Otherwise all I can offer is a lifelong love of the theatre and the journalist's passion for finding out how things are done.

Whether directors nowadays have too much authority is a debatable point, and I have not enjoyed in the least eccentric and wildly gimmicky productions, in which the director seems to stand in front of everything else, including the text, and scream, 'Look at me.' Shakespeare, especially, comes in for a hammering.

The book does not pretend to be a comprehensive guide to contemporary theatre directors; it is a brief survey of a group of these working in the theatre today, whose work has given me pleasure. I would hasten to add — as anybody who knew me in my reviewing days will vouch — that this does not mean that I have sat through every play directed by every one of these directors in a state of glassy-eyed admiration.

I yawned my way through *Candide* at Stoke, and *Zorba the Greek* at Greenwich. I sat bemused and inattentive during *Veterans* at the Nottingham Playhouse, and I hated every minute of the 1974 *King John,* which I found a nightmare of overlong self-indulgence. But virtually all the productions I have discussed here with their director appealed to me immensely, from the stunning Brook *A Midsummer Night's Dream* through Michael Blakemore's *Long Day's Journey into Night* to David Jones's *Love's Labour's Lost,* which gave me one of my happiest nights at the theatre, and made me laugh so much my ribs hurt the next day. Laughter like that is rare. To more than balance the failure of *King John,* there was John Barton's *Twelfth Night* and *Richard II.* But whether a Cheeseman documentary like *The Knotty* or an unusual production of Shakespeare like Trevor Nunn's *The Winter's Tale* appeals to you is purely subjective. As I have said many times, theatre criticism or appreciation can only ever be one person's view because the human mind is not a computer. *Ex cathedra* statements on the theatre do not appeal to me.

The piece on Joan Littlewood differs from the other contributions because she is fighting for survival, unlike the rest of these directors. The reasons for this are too complex to go into quickly, but are a national disgrace.

I am grateful that whatever it was that I was born with, it included the gift described by Patrick Garland (quoting Auden) as 'a sense of theatre', even if in my case it was a sense of enjoyment rather than of participation. I owe a great deal to my parents — to my mother, who introduced me to theatre through the ballet, and to my father, who would finish a shift in the pit on a Friday night and then go on a three-hour cycle ride with me to Stratford to queue for standing tickets for a play. This love of make-believe and illusion, the enchantment of the theatre, survived through all kinds of problems, even when life was at its bleakest. We are, I suppose, as David Mercer said in *Duck Song,* just 'fools under the stars all the time'.

I would like to thank all the secretaries and press office staff in theatres, especially Bill Allen and Peter Harlock of the RSC and Craig Macdonald of the National Theatre, also Judi Dench, who kindly wrote the foreword after reading the manuscript. Needless to say, I am very grateful indeed to all the directors who gave up a considerable amount of time to the project, and treated it with enthusiasm. My thanks too to Jan who typed my appallingly annotated copy, and last but not least to Philip Hedley — to whom I have dedicated this book — for his continual encouragement.

A small amount of the material first appeared in either *The Birmingham Post* or the *Guardian.*

# Contents

# John Barton

In any discussion with theatre directors you will hear John Barton described as *the* text man, the person who above all others wrings every atom of meaning out of Shakespeare's texts. He is also described sometimes as a kind of academic manqué who came into the theatre almost by accident, and is really pining to go back to university cloisters, but this is not how he sees himself. He is, however, a man who finds it difficult to communicate his ideas, which is why he dislikes intensely being directly quoted.

He feels that it was only by a freak of fate that he went into the academic life at all. He had always wanted to go into the theatre, but when in due course he was offered a Fellowship he took it. However, it was all rather a mistake, and when Peter Hall asked him to come to Stratford-on-Avon he was really somewhat relieved to leave Cambridge.

There is always an initial academic approach to his work, however unobtrusive this might be, which provides the groundwork to the finished production. He begins working on a play, like many other people, just reading and rereading the text, although he will do this more than many of his colleagues. As his assistant, Penny Gold, says, 'He will read it over and over again until he can tell you where any line comes, unlike those people who have to turn the pages over to find what's said in the next speech even in the rehearsal room. He does emphatically know more than most directors about the text. There are very few questions an actor can ask John that he cannot completely, honestly and assuredly answer from that text. He's not bluffing his way through, which is very reassuring for the actor.

'Having started off with the text, he then goes on to read a great deal of related material — for example, for *King John* he read possible source and related plays, such as Bale's *Kynge Johan* and the anonymous *The Troublesome Raigne*.

The stage version incorporated much of both these plays and other fragments connected in some way with John. He does a good deal of critical background reading as well, although that's not something he advertises in the rehearsal room.

'Always the ultimate sanction is the text. People might say to him "Can't we do so and so?" and he'll say no, because the text doesn't allow it, but that isn't the same as saying the text is the Holy Bible. He believes in the theory of continuous copy, the idea that Elizabeth texts were constantly modified to fit the varying conditions of individual performances. He therefore doesn't take the text as completely inviolate. His approach to one of his latest productions, *King John*, is consistent with this theory, as he feels that the play, as an early work, has areas of uncertainty, areas where potentially powerful nuances are not picked up — when the Faulconbridge brothers present King John with their rival claims to their father's inheritance, which are based on a will, John shows no uneasiness in arbitrating this mirror image of his own uncertain claim to the throne of England.

'As he said in his programme note, "Whenever I have seen *King John* on the stage I have been fascinated yet perplexed. When I read it again at the end of 1973, I was struck by how much the play, probably written in 1594, is about England and us *now*. Our world of outward order and inner instability, of shifting ideologies and self-destructive pragmatism, is also the world of *King John*. Even the specific political issues have modern parallels, although I have never seen this emerge fully in performance. So I turned to *The Troublesome Raigne of King John* (Shakespeare's possible source play, 1591) and to the earlier *Kynge Johan* (1539) for clues as to why.

"I found that those areas left cloudy by *King John* were more clearly explored in *The Troublesome Raigne*, which develops into full speeches, or even scenes, things that in Shakespeare are unexplained references. It appeared that a marriage of the two texts might be fruitful.

"John Bale's *Kynge Johan* uses the moral absolutes and the bold dramatic pattern of a medieval morality play to uphold a fiercely political Protestant polemic. The step from *Kynge Johan* to *The Troublesome Raigne*, though great, is direct, and even *King John* has strong morality ingredients. But *King John* has cast off much of the striking formality of its medieval forerunners without, I feel, wholly replacing it with the flexible subtlety of Shakespeare's mature work. The cruder *Troublesome Raigne,* on the other hand, retains the sharp traditional pattern. I felt it would be valuable to bring to a production of today some of the starkness of the medieval style which can speak so clearly to a modern audience in this age of Brecht, Arden and Edward Bond.

"So, with these points in mind, I finally decided to make some additions to the text, using elements from both the other King John plays. I would never consider tampering with mature Shakespeare — it is stylistically inimitable — but this early work has much of the poetic tone common to many plays of the 1590s, and some lines from *The Trouble-some Raigne* are not incompatible with Shakespeare's text.

" 'The idea of adapting a play to set free its voice is not new: Shakespeare's *King John* has left several directors uneasy and led them to make additions from the sources. In a sense, any production of a play is an adaptation of the original. As soon as a director perceives a particular meaning, and begins to explore it and define it, he is inevitably committed to selecting, focusing and rejecting alternatives. But a production cannot help creating as well as criticizing, so turning the original text into something it is not by itself. Having started with very limited plans for cuts and insertions, I found that despite myself, as I worked, and as rehearsal progressed, new leads and possibilities emerged, and these led me to much wider textual changes and additions than initially envisaged. Our final version incorporates many lines from *The Trouble-some Raigne,* a few from Bale's *Kynge Johan,* some medieval carols and additions of my own. I hope and believe that my additions do no more than develop and clarify tendencies already in the three plays from which this version is drawn." '

He sees little theatre himself, but as Penny Gold says, 'It's amazing how much he makes use of his very limited external theatrical experiences. You can't think of anything more · separate from *Richard II,* for example, than *Private Lives,* yet that influenced his production, in its formality, the game-playing that goes on between the characters in the play, the

degree to which they are all very conscious of the roles that
they are supposed to play, the way they act up to those roles
but at the same time have a distance to them. All this, he
felt, was analogous to the position of Richard. I'm not saying
it had a profound influence on the production, but the fact
that it had an influence at all is significant.'

He worked on *Richard II* for a long time, as he had done a
Theatregoround version of the play in 1971. He became more
and more concerned with 'the King's two bodies' — that is,
the parallel between King and actor, both of whom are
required to perform before an audience, and both of whom
have to submerge their individuality to the role.

One of the most effective innovations in the production
was when the groom who visits Richard in prison turns out to
be Bolingbroke. He says, however, that he did not intend this
to be taken literally — like so much else in the production, it
is an image which is given dramatic form. Richard, as the
divinely appointed King, is trapped in his role, and inhibited
by it from true contact with other, merely mortal, men. Only
when in prison, uncrowned, can he speak simply as a man.
Bolingbroke too, as soon as he becomes King, is trapped, but
he, unlike Richard, was not groomed for kingship, and
therefore feels the weight of the restrictions the crown
imposes on him very early in his reign. This realization of the
role-playing his position demands, and his inner sympathy
with Richard, finds an expressionistic, if not realistic, outlet
in his visit to the prison. The King is there, naked of his role,
dressed in a prison garment; Bolingbroke as the groom can
confront him similarly naked. Thus stripped the two men
are enabled to say those things which in the outside political
world were disallowable.

With Ian Richardson and Richard Pasco alternating in the
roles of Richard and Bolingbroke, the production becomes,
intentionally or not, two very different plays. The Ian
Richardson performance was far more political, making
Richard continually prone to self-dramatization, an unlikeable person heading for a deserved fall, whereas Richard
Pasco was more emotional, and you felt far more sorry for
the character. They were equally valid, and I wondered if the
difference in characterization was intentional, but John

Barton said virtually the same thing to both actors.

The character becomes different as it is interpreted through the different personalities of the actors. The force of any line is modified by the actor who speaks it; the words said by Ian Richardson can sound quite different when spoken by Dickie Pasco. It isn't wholly a directional thing, but essentially springs from what the individuality of an actor brings to a role, something which always exists in the theatre but which isn't usually so noticeable when actors do not alternate in parts.

Kingship fascinates him, and, of course, the title of his anthology on the life and death of kings, *The Hollow Crown,* is taken from *Richard II.*

> within the hollow crown
> That rounds the marked temples of a king
> Keeps Death his court, and there the antic sits . . .
> As if this flesh which walls about our life
> Were brass impregnable; and humour'd thus,
> Comes at the last and with a little pin
> Bores through his castle wall, and farewell king.

The anthology has proved popular, he thinks, because what it really sums up is the vanity and mortality of kingly glory, and, even though much of the mystique has passed away, it is that glory that people, in some strange way, still feel.

Another historical production of his which fascinated me was *Henry V,* which he directed for Theatregoround. I sat in a school hall in Walsall on a wet night and watched about a dozen actors, dressed in jeans and jerseys, perform the play, doubling the French and English armies, and the effect was so impressive that the whole audience would have risen as a man and followed Henry into the breach. He had worked on the play, either acting, directing or broadcasting it about nine times, and each time he did it there seemed to him to be yet another way of doing it. The simplicity of style with a small cast and no elaborate scenery is wholly fitting to a play which is held together by a chorus which constantly says, 'let's pretend'.

Away from kings, there was his production of *Othello,* set in the mid-nineteenth century, where the characters looked as if they were moving inside an old sepia photograph. Here he was most ably interpreted by Julia Trevelyan Oman, who is steeped in the period and who matched his concept totally. Again, in *Twelfth Night* the visual images stay in the mind; the autumnal colours, the flickering candles, the atmosphere of the sea. Yet he has never worked regularly with any one designer, although in the early stages of doing a production the designer is the person to whom Barton, as a director, talks most.

Basically, John Barton is a person who is never satisfied with what he does. He always wants to remake things; when plays are transferred they tend to be entirely remade. He always talks in terms of getting things right, although he would deny that there was any such thing as a definitive interpretation of anything. Yet, as Penny Gold says, he frequently says, 'I got that bit right,' or 'He got that right,' or 'He didn't get that bit right,' as though somewhere there is an answer. He feels he got more of *Twelfth Night* 'right' than most things. There is always a dichotomy between his feeling that he has got something right and his principle that nothing is definitive, but it is difficult to put any of these concepts into words. Like most people who work in the theatre, he feels that even something as verbal as Shakespeare becomes limited when defined by words. What happens on the stage is not just a feeble interpretation of the text but is something larger and more comprehensive. The priority for him must be that something actually works on the stage.

# Peter Brook

Without doubt the biggest single influence on the work of British directors over the last ten years has been that of Peter Brook. As John Trewin says, 'His career has been visible thinking aloud. For him yesterday in the regular theatre is always dead except as a post-mortem subject.' The young lion whose talent was picked out by Sir Barry Jackson, and who embarked on his first Stratford production, *Love's Labour's Lost,* with a box of cardboard figures with which to work out the moves, has become the man endlessly searching for new forms of theatre, for new responses from new audiences. When he emerges from a period of search to produce something like the RSC's *A Midsummer Night's Dream,* then the results can be staggering.

During the last three years he has been working at the International Centre of Theatre Research which he founded in Paris. The work he did there is uppermost in his mind, and it is on that work that he is building for the future.

'Well, what we've been doing through the conditions of the Centre is to work in a wider variety of conditions, more freely than would have been possible without it. I don't think I've ever felt, in any production I've done, a pressure to do other than what the work needed, so I can't think of a case where I felt that a production has been less experimental. In a sense, I don't understand the division between experimental and non-experimental work. It's a stupid attitude to think that you put on a different hat and do more experimental work one day than the other; so, in a sense, one looks in a production to bring it as close as possible to what would be true, so I've never resented any conditions that I've been in because each condition — which was the main point I tried to make in *The Empty Space* — has its negative and positive sides. If you're forced to do a production in two days, this needn't be a calamity — it can be marvellous. When you know you only have so many possibilities, this can be exciting. It is also often a terrible constraint, and can be very destructive, but the truth is always in a combination of the two.

'There are certain things which are just impossible under certain conditions. For instance, if you have to do a production in so many weeks in a certain theatre in a certain language for a specific social class, then you are free within those conditions, but you are not free not to do the play or suddenly to decide to do a different one at the last second. This isn't as frivolous as it sounds. For instance, I took on the obligation to do the *Dream* for the RSC at a certain date. I'm not free the night before to say we're not going to do it, we're going to do an improvization on Kissinger and Nixon. I'm not free to do that because of obvious structures — such as thousands of seats have been sold to tourists who have come across the world knowing through their travel agents that they are going to the theatre to see a certain play. All those common-sense elements are not pressures, they are facts. There is an anarchic wish which often arises to ignore those facts and say right, we'll have a happening, you'll come to the theatre expecting to see the *Dream* but in fact you'll see something totally different. There are moments when that has to be done, and has been done. But obviously, as a way of living, you work within the existing conditions and make the best of them. For this reason there is a set of things which have to be taken for granted; such as, an actor learns a part and he gives three months' study to it; to pull it away from under his feet at the last second because you think it will be more interesting to see it turned inside out is something that you don't do in work that is conditioned to fit within the system where once everybody has accepted the responsibility to produce a certain result, they set out to produce it.

'That carries with it more assumptions than you would imagine, because the moment you accept that responsibility — and I don't mean you individually, but you as a whole group of people — it means that you accept the place — the relation with the audience, the special economic relations, the human relations, all those things that are the quintessential theatre. You obviously condone and accept

these, which means that you are not free to work drastically outside those conditioning factors. It is no use refusing some of these factors and not others: if you step outside you must do so totally, which was why we had to build the Centre.

'The whole of the work we've been doing over the last three years began with what I thought was a major experiment which we did with the *Dream* in rehearsals which you might have heard about. Two weeks before it opened we went and played it in Birmingham at the Midlands Arts Centre, and the reason for this was first of all in the nature of the play. I wanted everybody to understand that it was the actors always playing and improvizing, it was never a production fixed by a director in a certain way for the actors to obey. I wanted a context in which the actor could continually come back remaking the play, and to make this live is a very difficult idea of improvization — it isn't total freedom, nor is it total restriction with discipline, it is something mysteriously blending the two. It's hard to analyse, and important to feel very deeply.

'We made a lot of experiments, of which the major one was to take a production that was getting set in a certain form because that form was necessary for the theatre in which we were going to play it, and play it without any of those elements, purely from the spirit and not the form. So that although we'd been working for ten weeks with juggling, swings, sticks and plates, and had been working in a very precise space with a very definite relation to an audience at the Stratford Theatre, we went out to Birmingham taking no props, no accessories of any sort, with the actors working from what was at that moment their living knowledge of the play after that much rehearsal. The improvization was an improvization to find, on the spur of the moment, the outside forms that made this shared sense come to life for the people who were there. It was a tremendous occasion for everyone, because it was the first time we had seen the *Dream* alive in the way we'd been working on it.

'Afterwards what was clear was that although this free version was marvellous, if you put that sort of version into the vast areas of Stratford it wouldn't mean anything. It lived because it was in a space not much bigger than this room here, and everyone was sitting around. It was personal, simple, human.

'When David Waller made his first entrance as Bottom he'd been sitting leaning against a wall, and had fallen asleep behind *The Birmingham Post.* Everyone looked up when that voice suddenly came from behind the paper, and there was a man in a cloth cap, and it was Bottom. It was marvellous off the cuff among three hundred people but very self-conscious if you suddenly stuck that on to a glaringly lit platform. It was quite clear that this technique was absolutely true in Birmingham and absolutely false in Stratford. It's a tremendous question, because either one asks — wrongly — which is the truer, or one says both are true, and if you'd taken bits and pieces from the large theatre thirty miles to Birmingham and had tried to rig up a Stratford version of it it would have been neither fish nor fowl. If we had tried to do what was living in Birmingham, in its more liberal context, in a situation which demanded formality, then that would have been equally false; formality is a tool at Stratford because in a sense formality on that stage *is* a tool which permits intense communication with a thousand people. It's a different game with different rules. I think the only way of looking at it is in terms of games and rules. Like in a game two or ten players start to establish a certain thing by the end of the game, but when the rules constantly change you have to assess each time what the local rules are, and not play the wrong rules in the wrong place.

'After that we did the same experiment again in the Round House, and again it was a tremendously important experiment for everyone in the organization — for Trevor's *Hamlet,* Terry's *Richard III* and the *Dream* — to see what is theoretically called a production. The word is used very loosely — a director used to be called a producer, he produces and he makes a production, but in that production there are two aspects which happen separately. There is the inner production and the outer. The inner is the understanding, the intellectual and living understanding of what it's all about, what you're doing and why you're doing it. And that passes through rehearsal into the actor's bones, and the actors have a living knowledge of what the play is all about. That you can't take away from them. You can clothe them differently, but it remains. The other production is what the director in another hat and the designer do, and this production either submerges the play if it's over-decorated, or if it's dead right, it is the tool by which the inner production's intentions are communicated.

'But the outer production always belongs to a place, so that if you leave the place it isn't a question of whether you believe in the proscenium theatre or not; if you have accepted to play within a proscenium theatre, then you have to find the solutions, which are often very difficult to find, but which make it possible for something to live in a proscenium theatre. The moment you go away from that you are under no obligation to carry out any of it with you. Going from Stratford to the Round House, we established that the physical production (which was highly important at Stratford, and couldn't just be thrown out of the window or the play wouldn't have lived on that stage) belonged to that place only. And as a show going on tour doesn't think of carrying the seats, the box office and the usherettes with it, in the same way if you are touring and not going to identical theatres like we did on the world tour you can leave behind everything but the internal work.

'Now, coming out of this, when the *Dream* went on tour, at the same moment I was involved in two tours. There was the *Dream* which I was deeply attached to, going around the world, and there was the group from the Centre which is equally part of my work, going through Africa — and the two couldn't have been more different. The *Dream,* to go on tour, had to accept and play the game by certain rules, those rules being first of all that being a language play it would play to audiences who would either follow the language to a large degree or be interested in making the effort to penetrate a play which is densely verbal. The other thing was that through the structure and economics of world tours of big companies, the RSC and British Council and all that, the RSC were condemned to go to middle-class showcases in the major cities, going from comparable slot to comparable slot, rather like carrying Stratford around the world.

'I'd originally wanted to do performances of the *Dream* outside those conditions. For instance, there was for a long

time negotiations for it to go to Shiraz when we were there
with the Centre. At Shiraz I'd found a teahouse, a marvellous
little place with a duck-pond in the middle of it, and a broken
wall where people could sit on cushions and carpets in the
yard with the ducks walking round them from the pond and
with a plank across. The way we could have done the *Dream*
there would be marvellous — in teahouse terms the equivalent
of Birmingham, but as the *Dream* had to go off on this vast,
respectable prestige tour, for better or worse it had to repeat
itself. In the end for the worse, because the actors had to do
their duty rather than what came from life. It's sentimental
to talk about it, and anyway the actors were pleased to be
part of something which earned a lot of money and was a
big deal, so that half the reason why people went was to set
themselves up for a year financially, and the other reason was
to see the world, so they felt their obligation was to repeat
the show as well as possible. I think that everybody in the
show would have been more excited if all those secondary
things had gone out of the window and we could have done
all kinds of different and exciting adaptations of it, playing
it to Esquimaux, Mexicans. It would have been more satisfying to us, less so to the people in authority who need to keep
that kind of glamour circuit going.

'One can't reform — nor is it my business to change things
on that scale. So what I attempted to do was to play the
game according to the rules and make the best of it, going
around with the *Dream* and re-rehearsing it all the time to
try and keep it alive but with the second group. I was doing
the kind of work which only begins when you can play where
you want, when you want and where absolutely no set of
circumstances lays down anything whatsoever except the self-
imposed obligation to do your best, rather than your worst,
work when the time comes.

'That is a long, tangled road, but that is what the Centre
is about. It is all about saying it was necessary for a lot of
other people and myself to look for theatre outside the rules,
self-imposed or otherwise, and when we set up the Centre the
one condition, the one factor we used to talk about to people
I hoped would back us, and who expected me to make long,
complicated artistic statements about our aim, was that the

basis of the work was that it should be totally subsidized. It might not sound very dramatic but in fact it was, because I realized, through living so much through the destinies of the RSC, that even with a big subsidy a company must always earn a large proportion and make most of its money through the Box Office. In a sense, total freedom doesn't exist even with a high subsidy; total freedom exists when the subsidy means that you need never work at all, and that was the ideal circumstance I wanted, that we could put ourselves in a position of total luxury where some unknown benefactor could set us up to sit and do absolutely nothing, recognizing that once that situation was created there were the conditions of a research laboratory. Then you work out of compulsion, out of need, out of love, out of all sorts of reasons. In fact, you end up working very hard. For instance, in Africa we travelled something like five thousand miles in ninety days, and in that ninety days we rehearsed, we travelled non-stop, and we played about thirty times. In Brooklyn we played an enormous number of times, for we played in the Brooklyn Academy in the evenings, we played in the streets and locality twice during the day, and we'd have working meetings with other groups. Working in this way compared with that of normally constructed companies, you were always in a position to be able to choose the place, time and content. So as we'd no obligation to lure an audience we didn't have to have a title for what we did nor repeat the same thing.

'Within the traditional set of rules by which, on a certain night, you deliver something, the work itself is basically a two-phase operation. Phase one is preparing, phase two, performing. In that it's like any manufacturing process — and I don't mean that in a pejorative sense — or like a studio artist where for a long time something is prepared, prepared, prepared, then at a certain moment it is finished and delivered, shown, made available, offered for sale. It is that two-stage process which is the basis of everything, from handicrafts to painting a picture for an exhibition. When you relate this to the theatre it means that the audience belongs to phase two, and a lot of what's good and a lot of what's dead in our theatre comes from that conception, out of which comes the

feeling that the audience is a separate element which was
introduced or injected at a later stage. This enables you to
do what so many groups have done recently — and I think it
is suicidal — and that is to drop the audience completely. In
other words, to make phase one a way of life. Very understandable, even intellectually understandable, because in a
sense the audience belongs to a later stage, and in a sense
corrupts or spoils what is perfect in its own right. But the
moment you abolish the two phases everything becomes
phase one. Then the audience is a factor from the second
the work of creation begins, and this leads to quite a different
result.

'So in a sense I can say our work has been returning to the
source of theatre, although I don't like the phrase because of
the notion that returning means going backward; you can
return to a source by going either backward or forward. If
you look at what is the source, say, of a coal fire, the moment
you stoke it up you don't have to look anywhere else than
where the coal is glowing. If the source of a dramatic
experience is within the event, then one road is to prepare
and prepare and prepare until the event takes place, and the
other way is not to lose sight of the fact that however you
prepare for it, what you are talking about only lives in that
event. And, as you know, this is something I have been
rotating towards for a long time, but through the Centre it is
possible to come much closer to it. The theme of all our
work is what is happening now at the moment of performance
— but using many different forms and trying to understand
three questions. What has to be improvized, what has to be
prepared, and what mustn't be prepared? Because it's not
true to say that improvization happens by itself; it doesn't.
It has levels of quality — it's as simple as that. One talks
about improvization as though all improvization is the same,
but there is good and bad. The bad happens when conditions
are not right, the good when they are. Exactly like cooking —
bad cooking takes place when the mixture is badly made.
Cooking is a subject where people have a far more common-
sense approach than theatre.

'If you put in front of someone who says that in the
theatre all that matters is complete freedom of expression, a

rottenly cooked, uneatable stew, he'll say, "What *have* you done — this is disgusting!" If you say — as an actor often does — "That's how I felt it. So I put in vinegar because I felt it, but the milk curdled so I added sugar because I felt that way", and so on, they'll think you're barmy. Rightly. Improvization is no more like haphazard feelings coming together than if you mixed milk and sugar. It makes a mixture — but it would be meaningless, unpalatable, and a repellent mixture. Good cooking is also an improvization, but it isn't automatic, surrealist behaviour, it's an alive, creative way of making something through improvization knowing that if it is done rightly something of quality will emerge. There is a science to improvization, and the science is what makes the difference between the bad and the good. We know so little about it — and our work is to help us learn. All the arts have the same problem, in music, in ballet, in painting.

'Our general rules are so rotten that it's necessary to find the deeper chain of rules; then something happens according to the rule, not in a restrictive but in a supportive way, because the guidelines are there. In the theatre it is absolutely vital for us not only to have all the theatre freedoms I've talked about but also the social freedoms to be in touch with a different sort of audience. This, I'm afraid, can only be put in a very cold-blooded way. If you believe that every human being, without exception, has a natural right to be part of an audience, and if you reject the whole notion of selecting an audience and having an imaginary passport at the door where you say I don't want you, I don't like your face, one realizes that an audience is whoever wants to come. It is then obvious that the work we are talking about is for everyone. Unfortunately, the cold-blooded point is that for the research we want to do everyone is equal except people who normally go to the theatre — because all over the world theatre-goers contain a high proportion of those who through going to the theatre accept its crumbling conventions.

'So that in a way, although the theatre-goer can have many free responses, in the sort of research *we* were doing the person who has a set of already established responses hasn't got the one thing we were looking for — the possibility of

responding absolutely directly to the event. That's why we
went far afield to explore with people who did not know
about theatre. In going to Africa we were looking, not for
some imaginary African innocence, but because in Africa
there was no recognition of Western theatre conventions. The
event had to justify itself, live or die, on strictly human
terms, and of course we were dealing with people with an
unbelievable capacity for human response. If we approached
them on a level that they respected they would respond with
respect, but they wouldn't give us one second's glance through
respect for theatre conventions. It was an overwhelming
experience. The actual theatre language had to be made up
each time.

'At the start of the work of the Centre we had to make it
clear to our sponsors that we are not going to build any form
of institution, so that I gave it this name so that it would
clearly not be considered a theatre company. If it's a
company people would say what's the show, when are the
performances? On the other hand, the name International
Centre of Theatre Research carried with it something that it
was necessary to break down straight away. That was the
impression that it was a place with a reading room and a
library and people writing to ask what were the qualifications
of admission. It isn't that at all — it's a group of people
working with a minimum of accessories. So we have a minimum of staff and an unbureaucratic way of working: no time-
table, and all the work is practical.'

What, I asked him, of all the dreary, meaningless so-called
'experimental' theatre we see, the kind where audience participation can actually mean the audience being injured? Is there
not a danger of this outlook being misunderstood?

'It's unfair today to separate anything from its social cause.
For centuries we've been building up a more and more absurd
society. The whole of society is absurd, but because one's
become accustomed to it one relapses into taking this absurd
society as being normal. Yet this society can create moments
of refusal so intense that the rebel finds such absurd outlets
as streaking — streaking looked at objectively is a total
absurdity, but then so is the anti-streaking society with its
magistrates and the whole machinery of state. Doing someone

else physical injury in the theatre expresses a total misunderstanding. Theatre is a field where there shouldn't be physical danger simply because the great power of the theatre only comes when everyone feels secure, trusting it's just make-believe, so that on a much deeper and much more thrilling level real dangers can be met. It's a funny thing, safety and risk go hand in hand, so though it's difficult to make a general definition, I think that one of the axioms of the theatre, something that is fundamental, is the notion that it's an imitation, that it isn't the real thing. It is the life and yet it isn't. This contradication is what the whole business is about. If half of the contradiction goes, we get life all right, but we lose the special intensifying of life that theatre can bring.

'At the moment I'm deep in preparations of different sorts for the next period of my work. I need very much to apply the work of the Centre to some large-scale public work. In other words, to return to the scale of the *Dream* because it has always been necessary for me to combine these two extremes, what you can explore and look for on a very small scale, and also to have an outlet that involves large numbers of people, which are socially generous. It's overwhelming to think of the Greek theatre, the physical fact of fifty thousand people all living around an event, where something was spreading into life and back from life because of the openness of the event and the fact that a lot of people were seeing it. Certainly the next period is going to be bringing the work together in forms that are more accessible. It is necessary to take the risk of putting experiments to the test. To go back to that improvization we did in Birmingham before the *Dream* — it was thrilling, but it wasn't half as difficult as doing the play on the big stage.

'I think this is something that groups working in freedom don't want to know about. Having worked on both sides of the fence, I know only too well the temptation to over-estimate the quality of what one is doing. It's easy to get a satisfactory result in easy conditions. There is something marvellous about a family charade game where everyone laughs at the five-year-old. But it is easier to play with the family than to make something that will touch the humour and intelligence of people all over the world.

'There is something that can only be discovered in small-scale theatre work — but then this needs to be translated to the wider challenger, the wider scrutiny of big-scale events.

'People ask me what we've learned, and of course there is no answer because you don't learn things. It is a meaningless question, the sort uncles put to children when they don't know how to make conversation and say "What did you learn today"?

'I don't think with all the glimpses we have had one can evolve any kind of theoretical statement. What one learns is something very different, and is common to all learning processes. You reach new points of no return. By this I mean that if once you have had the taste of how marvellous it is to play to an audience of the vividness of human response that you have in Africa, then you cannot accept playing in a cold, barren theatre with an audience with pallid responses. A new standard is created that you then have to respond to — you've reached that point of no return, having seen the best.

'We did a Peter Handke play, *Kaspar,* first of all as an exercise, painstakingly and slavishly as the author had written it, which was good for us as it forced us to be precise. But we found we could communicate the play in that way only to a tiny cross-section of humanity, because it can only be played to an equally small number of people who can mentally make themselves ready to take on a Handke set of rules; for those able to listen to language exactly on Handke's wavelength it was fine, but for those who are not, for a million legitimate human reasons, if only because it was written for a particular social class in the language of the intelligentsia, then those people are not going to make the first step to come into tune with it. The barrier couldn't be in any way breached.

'So we found we had to change the form until in the end Handke's austere and verbal play became a musical with very little dialogue (half the words went entirely), movement, dancing, songs, and eventually we came to a fine version that could scoop in any audience — and then what the play was about came to life. Handke saw both versions and liked the free one much better. The inner content matters, the outer form matters — but it is the coming to life of the inner content that matters most of all.'

# Peter Cheeseman

In terms of sheer amount, I have more material written by Peter Cheeseman than by any other director. Immensely articulate, with an ear for the media, he loves putting his ideas on paper and explaining his beliefs to all who will listen. Somehow or other, he will make the headlines even if it is at a Council of Repertory Theatres conference where he castigates the theatrical delegates for sitting around scoffing trifle when they should be getting on with the work, or the local councils who feel all theatre people are just 'long-haired lettuce-eating buggers'.

Talking to him in his cluttered office ('that heap of papers on the floor represents the theatre's archives'), is something akin to being confined with a Force 9 gale in a matchbox, and he talks about the theatre with a fervour and enthusiasm a Fundamentalist minister might use to bring you to God.

'No, I can't say I intended to go into the theatre to begin with. I wanted to be a chemist. I don't go along with those people who say they just can't do this or that, they're hopeless or impractical or something. It's pathetic, but in fact I just couldn't do the maths. I don't know why — it's not something to be proud of. My mother encouraged me to act in my teens, which I did with an amateur WEA group, and there I found an immense dedication, enthusiasm and sincerity lacking in the professional theatre. It was a shock when I did get into the profession and discovered 94 per cent of it is just rubbish, with people messing around and playing at it, and it was a very long time before I found the same kind of dedication there was in the best of those WEA groups and Unity theatres.'

Like other directors in his age-group, he did some work while he was in the RAF and began directing seriously at university (where his productions included an ambitious *King Lear*), and it took up a great deal of his time. ('Where is

Mr Cheeseman?' asked his tutor, 'Is he dead?') 'You can say I became a director for three reasons; because I wanted to go into the theatre, because I got stage fright and didn't really like going on to the stage, and because I fell in love with Jean Simmons and thought there you are, boy, get on with it, go into the theatre and you might meet her. (Never have . . . she'll never know how influential she was.)'

After the RAF he started looking for work. 'I did think about the BBC, but was warned by a number of people that if I once went there I'd never get out into the theatre.' After two years at Derby Playhouse he joined up with the late Stephen Joseph, and eleven years ago they found an old cinema in Stoke-on-Trent, and the Vic was born. 'It rated about one line in the local paper.'

Now theatregoers from all over the country and beyond make the trip to Stoke, which is not a pretty place, even though it is possible to have an immense affection for it. As one London reviewer remarked sourly when he arrived to review the Vic's *Hamlet,* the only place he could imagine bleaker than Elsinore was the outside of the Vic on a wet night . . . .

Cheeseman works always in the round, and his passionate enthusiasm for it is well-known. So much so that one April Fool's Day he did a radio item in which he said he would be providing Stoke's first open-air cinema in the round, and most people believed him.

'The first time I experienced real excitement at the physical arrangement of a theatre was in walking across our touring stage cloth when we set up the 1961 Centre 42 Festival at Wellingborough. Even in a really unprepossessing lash-up, theatre-in-the-round has for me all the rich potential that old-timers lavish on the dim darkness on the other side of the footlights' glare. The days of the bitterest contention about theatre forms seems to be past, but there's still more unknown than known about open stages. Our profession has developed centuries of sophisticated expertise in one uni-directional form, but so far we at Stoke are the only perman-ent company in Great Britain with any continuous history of working practice in any other, and it is a factor which affects so much of my work. I believe that theatre is a human activity that can survive and thrive anywhere — in the street, on the stairs, in a large cupboard under them. It is just that some arrangements are more efficient than others. I do not believe that any one form of theatre is any more *valid* than another. Those analyses or questions that speak of 'advantages' or 'disadvantages' of one theatre form as opposed to another are mistaken. The differences are of the same order as the difference between painting and sculpture, and you don't talk about the disadvantages of painting.

'I can express my own reasons for sticking to it. The simplicity and naturalness of the form has its own attraction. It is the form taken by real-life drama, at a fight in the play-ground, an accident in the street. The actor in the centre of the circle is totally exposed, totally vulnerable. He is also lonely, exceptional and therefore powerful. The community instantly formed by gathering in a circle is the sanction, the invitation to an important proposition. The ring of attention gives a special significance to every event that takes place within it. The circle itself has a permanent mystical and symbolic power, through usage, through tradition, through its infinite totality. And in the plain and simple action of looking across the circle at the drama in the middle and beyond it, we see human behaviour, the imitative rituals of our own lives enacted against a background which is, and represents, human society. Both the simple facts and the immediate imagery of theatre-in-the-round have a human potency which I find impossible to resist.'

His stated approach to the production of a play has a mind-bending simplicity, and it can only be partly true. 'You start with the text, and the only two things you have to do really are to cast it and design it — decide how it's going to look. That's all you need . . . once you've done that you've done your work. Casting isn't all that easy, though, in our sort of company because you have to think of all kinds of problems the average West End man never has to consider. He'll want such and such an actress, and his trouble will start if he can't get her because she's doing a film or something. Here, when I consider who to use, I have to think shall we use so-and-so, she's good and experienced but she's just played a major role, or shall we try this one who hasn't had to work too hard but hasn't really the experience, though she needs bringing on? I have to give a great deal of thought to balancing the cast, and what's best for the company.'

At no time has he gone in for what might be termed 'popular rep'. 'I think the idea that you can present crap to audiences and then wean them on to something you call cultural theatre is the biggest and oldest theatrical fallacy in existence. I can hardly believe it is in existence. If you put on crap, then crap-loving audiences will come. You must start as you mean to go on and then build on your creative merits. Don't imagine they'll come and see an Agatha Christie one week and then turn up to *Waiting for Godot* a few weeks later — they won't. We who work in the subsidized theatre carry a heavy responsibility because we use public money. If we put on rubbish, then we're ratting on that responsibility. Of course, people will come and see that rubbish if it is put on prettily, especially if they have no choice.'

His heart lies in the region, and he becomes annoyed at any disparagement, especially the idea that everything happens in London. 'It's like those letter-boxes in London marked Town and Country. Delegates at CORT conferences say "town" when they mean London. What do they think Birmingham, Wolverhampton and Stoke are — country? Do they see us all here mashing turnips or something or lying out in the sun on Balsall Heath before going to the village of Smethwick to see a play?' So Stoke has become famous for the Cheeseman documentaries, plays based on local happenings and local people, often using a great deal of music and solidly based on fact. *The Knotty,* the story of a local railway-line, *The Staffordshire Rebels,* about the Civil War, and even one on the founder of Primitive Methodism, *The Burning Mountain,* have all brought in audiences by the coachload.

For his documentaries he has developed his own way of working. He describes the process as 'a kind of inverted pyramid', which gradually involves more and more people. It begins with the research period, which can last anything up to six months, during which the chosen subject is investigated, first in books, then in original documents, diaries, letters, newspaper articles and, where possible, tape-recorded inter-

views with people who, for instance, worked on the Staffordshire railway or who were prisoners in the last war. Much of
the work he does himself, assisted by his resident dramatist,
'who operates under the strict discipline of not being
permitted to write any of the show himself'. In fact, everything used on stage, all words and actions, must be based on
primary source-material. 'The difference between starting on
a documentary rather than a play is that I've no idea who is
going to be cast as what, and we haven't even got a script.'
All the company members are given photocopies of the
research material, and at the rehearsals the mass of material
is gradually edited. The text of the play is created during
rehearsal, and sometimes members of the company take
charge of particular scenes or songs, rehearse them individually, and produce them in a rough form on the stage. As the
actors begin to work a scene begins to take shape, and dialogue is apportioned, business evolved, a production secretary
transcribes a first script for the scene and after much cutting
and modification the final script is arrived at.

Says Cheeseman, 'Usually after an agonizing final weekend
of doubt and uncertainty the show goes on, and is played in
our district in a kind of atmosphere of participation that is
almost impossible to describe. We have never made any
compromise in the direction of making shows comprehensible
to people from outside the district. There is no point — they
are our special contribution to its life, and any visitor who
drops in must expect to feel like a visitor. I believe myself
that an aim like that is likely to be much more creative than
one which seeks to please the nation, or the world. The only
human situations we can truly comprehend are the ones
small enough for us to feel ourselves a significant or
effective part. Otherwise our actual sense of existing at all
is expressingly diminished.'

Despite many offers to leave Stoke, he has turned his back
firmly upon London, and is the most vociferous spokesman
for regional theatres and how they should be built and run.
'Keep theatre cheap, or do we have to build the Taj Mahal?'
he asks in an article in *The Stage*. 'Once upon a time mayors
were happy with their names on a horse trough, nowadays
they'll settle for nothing less than a 1 000-seat civic theatre.'

Rightly, he concentrates on what should be put on inside,
not the magnificence of a building where the administrative
staff have to spend £7 000 a year to clean the windows alone.
On the wall of his foyer are graphs of little men, showing who
does what, and it is obvious that here, unlike many State-
subsidized theatres, the administrative staff do not completely
overwhelm the actors.

But when all this has been said, it must be pointed out that
he is one of the theatre's true theatrical innovators. You can
be furious with a Cheeseman production, outraged, angered
and exhausted, but never bored, and rarely disappointed. His
whale-hunt in his production of *Moby Dick* will stay in my
mind for life, and I can no longer believe that it was done by
half a dozen actors sitting on wooden boxes, because when I
think of it I can see the ship, the harpooner, the stormy seas
and the great white whale. This is what theatre is about. 'For
me', he says, 'to be a subsidized artist in a democratic
community is the most exciting thing one can possibly be.
I remember my former boss, Stephen Joseph, being asked at
a solemn forum what he felt should be the most important
feature of the new National Theatre building. "The most
important thing is to make it inflammable", he said, "so that
by the time they realize they've made a mess of the place it
can be burned down and they can start again." He was a great,
but serious, jester. When they give me my tin watch at sixty-
five I want to feel that might happen to the Vic. Rather that
than it should turn into a bloody great monument with my
name chiselled on it.'

# John Dexter

'Why did I go into directing? I went into it because there seemed to be nothing else I could do. It was as simple a reason as any.' John Dexter has a large work-load, and when I saw him he was just going to Paris to do an opera, then coming back to this country for *Pygmalion* in the West End, followed by *Romeo and Juliet* for the National and *Equus* in New York.

He is not a person who really enjoys discussing his work. 'I don't know how I work. I have no formula, and I don't know anyone who has. You read a play, you like it, you decide to do it, and you find a way of doing it. You read it until you know it as well as the author knows it, you talk to him about it, you cast it; it's a private process, in fact. It becomes public when you begin to work with the actors, and totally public when you come to show it to an audience, but that's the point at which I switch off from it. I don't like sharing it with the public that much — whether it's good or bad. That's my problem. Of course, I keep an eye on things once it's on, when it's running, but for me the real excitement ends at the last dress rehearsal. But as to a system, I haven't got one, I've never had one.'

The relationship between him and Peter Shaffer has been a fruitful and extremely successful one, and I asked him what attracted him towards Shaffer in the first place. 'He was there. Nothing *attracted* me towards Shaffer. He was an established playwright long before I was an established director. *The Royal Hunt of the Sun* had been kicking around between the RSC, the National, and the Royal Court for some time. It was lying around on Sir Laurence's desk, and I said I'd rather like to do this at Chichester and I went ahead and did it. The next one, *Black Comedy,* sprang out of that. I think John Bird was going to do it originally, but he dropped out and I happened to be in New York with Peter, working on something else, and we talked our way through it in New York. I came back to England with the first half finished and we went into rehearsal with a first half that was good and a second half that wasn't, and we gradually evolved that second half with Maggie and Albert in rehearsal.

'*Equus* was something that he had discussed with me first two and a half years ago. He showed me the first draft, we talked about it and worked on it, and from that came a second. At that time it wasn't intended that we should do it at the National, but Peter Hall thought we ought to, so we found a space for it and did it here. But I certainly didn't "pick on him". Nor does he come to me first with his ideas. He's a writer — he sits in a room with a typewriter. When he's finished it he'll discuss it with me and we'll discover if I have the idea of his intentions, try and get nearer to the structure that he wants, but I certainly don't influence what he's going to write. At least, I hope I don't.

'There have been plenty of playwrights who I haven't wanted to do, but who have been very successful. It's just a question of personal taste, which is sometimes to the public's taste and sometimes not. But that's not very important.'

From past experience I know that he has strong views on critics and how they react to that taste. 'They don't listen and they don't look. They have no eyes and they have no ears. They're unimportant. They have no long-term effect on one's ability to work. I think Noël Coward put it well when he said they may give you a bad breakfast but they won't interfere with your lunch. There are a number of irresponsible journalistic hacks (who you know as well as I do) around, who would really be better off as racing correspondents, but I doubt if they have sufficient information even on that subject. They certainly know nothing about the theatre or writing, as is evidenced by every word they write. Then there are some very serious and intelligent people who really care and take trouble; then again, there are those who take care and trouble but don't write very well. But on the whole I've got past being worried by them beyond an irritation that lasts a couple of hours, and I've discovered that they haven't really affected my choices of what I do over the years.

'They haven't all been successful choices — far from it. It

just happens that this year has been successful after a couple
of very unsuccessful years. It's up and it's down. I think one
of the best things I've ever done, for instance, was *A Woman
Killed with Kindness*, which was not a critical success because
what Jocelyn Herbert and I were trying to do wasn't understood at all. More important than that, the quality of the
writing wasn't listened to, understood or felt.'

He had just finished a production of *I Vespri Siciliani*. 'I
first did a production of this in Hamburg five years ago with
another cast and another company and it had considerable
success there. Rafael Kubelik, who is the GMD at the
Metropolitan, asked me if I'd like to go to the Met. and do
it but between the production in Hamburg and the Met.,
I've done six other operas. *Vespri* is one that I have a particular feeling for, because I think it's a very neglected work,
and a totally underestimated work musically. It's an opera
with a bad libretto and some musical patches where the
composer is marking time because of the libretto, but three-
quarters of it is first-class Verdi. I felt it needed an airing,
and that it needed a very positive angle, which I believe we
did.'

I asked him if he found directing opera singers more
difficult than straight actors. 'I'm very happy with them. I
can teach them something, they can teach me. As to their
being good or bad actors, I don't know what that means.
They only need, like actors, guiding.

'They're not different or difficult, they have massive
physical problems to deal with. Most actors can cut corners
if they can't breathe through a certain passage, but a singer
is totally exposed. There's no such thing as cutting a note.
If you did cut notes most people would recognize that you
had. So they are more exposed, more vulnerable, and greater
demands are made of them.'

What does he think of the old kind of opera production
where singers just stood there and sang without worrying
about any attempt at characterization? 'I was brought up on
the Carl Rosa where the standard of production was not of
the highest; and it was the same with straight plays, where
touring productions or repertory theatre was not the best,
but at least it's an education. Just because you pick up a

dirty, battered paperback of *Anna Karenina,* it doesn't mean
the book's bad, although it is always more of a pleasure to
read a well-bound, well-printed copy; but the material is still
the same.

'I've enjoyed the one really contemporary opera I've been
asked to do very much. Penderecki's *The Devils of Loudun*
is, I suppose, contemporary — at least, it was written only
five years ago. There's just another different set of problems
to solve. Is it difficult? *Everything's* difficult — not more
difficult; everything is bloody, fucking difficult. Everything . . .
There's no exception. Whether it's a three-handed play, a six-
hander, *Misanthrope, Devils of Loudun* or *Othello* — it's all
bloody difficult. There are always different sets of problems,
but the difficulties are always the same, and you can never
achieve what you are really aiming for. I can make the switch
between them because that's my job — that's what I do.

'It may be very wrong to diversify. I just know that I
enjoy doing it, and the hell with whether it's right or wrong.
Tyrone Guthrie managed to diversify without damaging his
ability to approach work truthfully, and I hope I can do the
same. He ran an opera company for years, and the Old Vic at
the same time at one point. He was a very, very remarkable
man. I think when you add up George Devine, Tyrone Guthrie
    totally opposite men, but totally dedicated and fully
theatrically trained and aware, with a passion for their job —
I haven't met anyone else with their particular energy and
knowledge and ability to teach and understand and make fun,
since they "left the building".'

How much influence does his designer have on him?
'Enormous — it's more important than casting the leading
role, because it's from the designer's response that you lay
out certain guidelines and make concrete your own ideas,
out of argument, out of discussion. This is why I really
don't like talking about work; all this presupposes a plan or
a system and there isn't one. I never have had. It's a question
of reading, looking round, doing the things you want to do.
Jocelyn Herbert's the designer I've worked with most.'

When I interviewed John Dexter originally he was feeling
very defensive about the National Theatre, saying that because
it was the National it was supposed to be doing the best work

all the time. 'That's absolutely true — everybody was having a
go. We were the worst thing that had ever happened. Now we're
fine, and last year it was the Royal Shakespeare's turn. These
things are in phases, and nobody outside the business ever
understands that it has to change all the time, it has to have
downward phases. Now we couldn't be in a more upward
phase — which is about the right time to leave. I shall do a
touring production of *Romeo and Juliet,* and put a couple
of productions into the South Bank, and then I want to ease
away a bit more. I think the new management should be able
to get on on their own, show their own taste, and I don't
intend to do much this year except revivals when they're
needed. I've been here ten years, and probably Tyrone
Guthrie was right when he said that five years was as long as
anyone could be creative in any one situation. By that count,
I've been here five years too long. There's a danger-point for
the institution and for me.'

Most of the directors are contemporaries of each other,
and there seems to be some feeling that there is not enough
talent coming along to replace them. John Dexter did not
agree. 'What do you mean, they don't have enough chances,
enough opportunities? Neither did I — so fuck 'em! You'll
find the Peter Gills, Michael Rudmans and Jim Sharmans
will get through. They're all doing the thing they want to
do.' I pointed out that many of today's established directors
were actually doing main productions in national theatre
companies in their twenties, whereas today's bright talent
tends to be on the fringe. 'But that's where it is — where do
you think the *The Infernal Machine* was done when Brook
directed it? Then he worked in repertory theatre — we've all
done it, there's no difference in the approach. But I think
the Royal Court needs Rudman or Sharman or someone to
go there. It's a natural progression. By the time we've dropped
into Tyrone Guthrie's grave, the other boys will be ready. It
happens in every profession. You begin, there's a middle and
an end — sometimes the end's early, sometimes late, but you
try and get as much work done between the beginning and
the end as you can. By the time I'm packing up, for whatever
reason, Rudman or Sharman or someone will be doing my
job and doing it better.

'When I was their age, Guthrie and Olivier were working together. Tennent, I suppose, controlled the West End. The structure's changed but it was the same group of people working, more or less because they knew each other, respected each other's talent and knew what they wanted to do. That happened with us, that will now happen with the younger generation. It's a process. Theatre is always in chaos, and it's always at a peak. There's a good supply of talent around, from what I've seen visiting around the fringe, and there will be plenty of opportunities for them because we shall all be falling by the wayside very shortly. But opportunity is usually made by disasters. It makes you realize you can't go on with the same old faces like me, Blakemore, Miller and Gaskill. We shall all do the things we want to do and leave space for the others.'

# Ronald Eyre

It isn't possible to type-cast Ronald Eyre, to say that this or that kind of play is what he does best, that he would be a good director within the framework of a national theatre company or that he has been most influenced by the Royal Court. His productions over the last few years have been too varied for this — *London Assurance, Much Ado About Nothing, Veterans, A Voyage Round my Father, Habeas Corpus, A Pagan Place,* have nothing in common.

'I think what I am trying to do all the time is to create a world in which a thing gets understood. I'm becoming increasingly used these days to finding that the reasons for doing or not doing any particular piece of work are becoming more and more obscure, not obscure to me but just generally obscure. I think it's because I'm not on any particular band-wagon. I rather like giving the impression that I'm in one place and then suddenly disappearing and not being traceable.

'I realize that from the outside this stance can look merely eccentric, so that what you say gets looked at as if it's eccentric too. So the difficulty is in creating a world where what you are doing is making sense to somebody, but without losing yourself in somebody else's world. I could have joined, say, the National years ago and gone along with whatever the current policy happened to be. But I felt that at that stage I would have been a courtier — and so far I'm not a courtier, I'm somewhere out on some other road. Perhaps some people have a life going on and work going on in two parallel lines but I don't work that way, and I don't think John Barton works that way either. What I'm interested in primarily is surviving, and in a limited sense blossoming. Work is very much living out life. In a way even doing productions has been a way of hiding because you have the companionship of the writer, whereas I now feel that I have to come out and be more totally responsible for a statement of whatever

kind. It will be ironical after all this if — as I suspect — the
statement can only be made in the context of some kind of
company with a more continuous commitment than one
production.'

He is not, he agreed, predictable. Recently he was asked
to redirect *London Assurance,* and after much thought, 'and
feeling from right down in the marrow', he refused. 'I was
under a good deal of pressure from old friends and from the
RSC and I was urged to do it, and the natural thing would
be, I suppose, to say yes, but it wasn't the natural thing for
me so I said no. Sometimes it takes me a long while to shake
off these pressures and do what may look to others like the
eccentric thing but which to me is the essential thing. I felt
that when I did Charles Wood's *Veterans* and dragged it up
and down the country.' *Veterans* had a terrible press when
it opened out of London, but was greeted with rapture
when it reached the Royal Court. 'You see, that's a case
where the world in which it first appeared wasn't created for
it. I never saw the first night at the Court, but I was told by
people who were there that it was one of the great first
nights. It wasn't because it was a different play by that time,
it was because it was breathing different air. I doubt, if you
put them in a capsule and examined the performance in
Nottingham and that at the Court, if you would see any
difference. It was just that they were being heard differently,
and so became different. It was a very difficult play — a
killer.'

Like most of his contemporaries, he came from a working-
class home. 'I suppose I went into the theatre because I was
the son of a depressed (in many senses) mining family in
Yorkshire. It was an escape. When you look back you can
see that theatre is not something you start late. I mean, you
don't go along to one of those juvenile employment ex-
changes and ask to be a theatre director, you know, because
a train driver gets sooty. It's way beyond that. The chance
to get away from or learn to handle the kind of life I was
looking at was absolutely via theatre. In those little houses
which are mostly draughts I would deal with the curtain
hanging at the back of the door instinctively; I was born
with it. I'm really an actor. The unease with things comes

out in the form of acting.

'So I started acting in Oxford, and acted a lot, but never knew what I was doing. I was an actor in blinkers; I may have been aware that an effect was being created but I couldn't see my way outside it in order to walk round it or explore it by manipulation. Take a case. Restoration Comedy. My first entrance. Came on stage, walked to the front and dried . . . and got a round of applause. I couldn't connect the failure with the effect, and I asked a friend what he'd seen, and he described how this evidently very confident man walked on and came to the front of the stage, and then a look of such extreme woe came all over his face that it was marvellous. Moments like that showed me that if I became an actor I might have to spend a lifetime as the victim of the audience. So I directed a few plays and realized that I could *join* the audience and get some of the pleasure of work on the stage as well, so that I could straddle the two things. I could be intelligent and evidently in control, not skidding.

'I think that coming from an untheatrical background has been an advantage. If you take *London Assurance,* for example, a person brought up in a theatrical background might have thought, well, my grandfather always said, "Make sure you have a person on either side of you and you can flick your head between them and you'll get a good laugh," which is a trad thing and very true. Donald Sinden knows all about the trad ways of getting an audience to react. But you see if I'd approached *London Assurance* that way it might have been just a demonstration museum piece, whereas it turned out to be a complete new world, almost a vision of paradise. It was where there was real good nature and people's pulse-rate was all right, flowers came out, and the trees blossomed and all that.'

I agreed with him that *London Assurance* had its own mad logic. 'It was good-natured. If you get to feel that no nature is ever good, or that everything has a sting in it somewhere and that's what makes it interesting, then here you have a place which *was* interesting but has terrible wholesome virtues. Talk about boredom! Not, I hope, on the stage, but within that society. Those endless days of doing a bit of stitching here or some writing there, followed by a little

chess-playing, yet they didn't seem to be climbing up walls.
They weren't all wanting to go to Moscow. They were all
right where they were. The difficulty about wholesomeness
like this is that it hasn't got to be put there on the stage
because it's good for you, the fellow who wrote it has to
feel that it's real. It's not a depleted world where things have
been hidden away because they aren't good for you to see —
a kind of maimed garden of Eden — the whole thing has to
be life as at that moment the playwright sees it, and at the
age of nineteen, which is what Boucicault was when he wrote
it I'm sure that's how he did see it and how he thought it
was, allowing for his astute sense of what would go down
well theatrically at Drury Lane. The play is crippled, though,
and was obviously written very headlong because he doesn't
get far enough fast enough. He's an act behind all the time,
and when he gets to the end of his penultimate act he should
have been there an act earlier. It isn't a classic in shape. He
doesn't tie it up properly, which is one of the problems for
a director doing it today, and I had to do a lot of rewriting,
because you've established that very leisurely pace only to
find yourself with a lot of loose ends and the curtain in
sight and no time to tie things up.'

He recognizes and admits his failures cheerfully. 'The first
play I ever did in London had a lovely set and some very
brave actors, but I wasn't entirely in tune with the play. Why
do that, then? Well, I'd worked in television, written a number
of things and felt I'd like to direct some theatre again just to
prove I could do it — and that was it . . . After that came
Donald Howarth's *Three Months Gone* at the Court, which
was pretty adventurous as it is a hellishly difficult play; it
only starts to work when you get to the point of seeing that
each person is a projection from one centre, so that when you
talk about identity and separation between characters it just
doesn't exist, as they merge into one another because the
person writing sees them all as rays of himself which sometimes shift and interlock and change colour.'

While some directors spend most of their time with the
national companies, others get labelled as 'Court' directors,
both tending to polarize. 'I don't want that polarization,
though because of that I'm probably out of favour with

everybody now. To me the Court is vigorous, and what I've
done there has been vigorous and vigorously fought over. I
especially enjoy their Theatre Upstairs, I've seen things I've
so much liked there — I've had more fun in that theatre
than any other place. There was the *Rocky Horror Show*
which was cheeky and good, then Klaus's play *Friday,* a
modest, well-carpentered play, and, of course, Mustapha
Matura's *As Time Goes By.* I just like sitting in that room
and seeing people do that kind of thing. I get pretty inhibited
being an audience in trad theatres.'

He had a successful production of *Much Ado* for the RSC:
'The only other professional Shakespeare I'd done was *Titus
Andronicus* at Birmingham. It was very, very difficult, and I
only realized how tired I was after the first week's rehearsal,
when I got back home and sat for six hours just breathing.
I enjoyed *Much Ado* more, and they've asked me to go back
a number of times, and I'd like to.

'But one of the problems of that theatre at Stratford is that
my style for a play like *Much Ado* would really have been
chamber style.

'If that cast had done that production in the Theatre
Upstairs it could have been ravishing. But at Stratford you
get that curious deformed barn to play in where even the
rehearsal room creates one thing and the theatre makes it
sound like another. It doesn't resonate. I don't know what
it is. I'm sure it's not by accident that a kind of ceremonial
method of performing Shakespeare happens in that theatre.
I found at Stratford that it was rather like having people
shriek Mozart up a wind tunnel . . . it was killing. When the
production got to London it was much more humane, it had
left behind that Stratford thing, "We stand in *line* and honk
it and none of us ever turns and faces anybody." I always
have the feeling of a headland on a windy day when I'm
there: bracing, but you've got to shout.'

Working so much with contemporary writers, does he have
much influence on the actual writing, on the finished result?
'Well, it varies from play to play. With *A Voyage Round My
Father* and John Mortimer he was busy doing lots of vivid
cases and he wasn't around much, but he was willing to
reshape things, and it became fuller as a result. In the case of

Charles Wood and *Veterans* he chisels his plays on quartz,
and what he writes is absolutely what he wants it to be, but
he is a very willing rewriter and lets you do it in a different
way, usually to prove yourself wrong. Come to think of it,
though, the text as printed after a show has opened is rarely
the text as it was when rehearsals started, and the text at
the start of rehearsals is rarely the text which first left the
playwright. But there's great variation in how much changes.
Take a play like *Habeas Corpus,* where the text changed
vastly. It was a rambling three-act play when I got it, and it
found its end-shape only by being worked on. But that was
a rare case. Usually – if it's a good play – the work goes in
a circle. You start from a point of non-understanding. The
writer lets you go on safari – may even come with you.
More often than not, you come back to the point you
started from.

'After that you start rehearsals, and how I start work
really does vary from play to play. I have no rules. That's
another reason not to do *London Assurance* or any other
play twice because your initial success cannot be repeated. What
happens the first time is you are there with your chemistry
(whatever that happens to be at that moment) and the
text, which is the result of somebody's nightmares, and
then there are the actors who have to be handled and loved
and so on, and you know that everything you do in a sense
will be against nature. Nobody *needs* the play to be done;
there's no crying necessity for it. You can just sweep the
stage and leave it empty: so everything you do is an act
against the state of things.

'Now what the process is by which you encourage this
and push and lure a lot of people to agree about the putting
on of a thing can't ever be done to a rule. There are cases,
for instance, like *London Assurance* where it might have
fallen down into a sort of coy sentimentality, so I had to
canter through it fairly briskly, making sure that nobody
condescended to the characters and that they were in fact
brisk, proper people. But even that's just today's way of
recalling what happened. I find it very difficult to recall
the real process. You see, you are in a hole when you are
doing a production. If you were Olympian, if you stood

above it, you could say, "Oh, yes, I know how it should be done, a couple of men there, a couple of women here, and it's all going to be lovely." Possibly there are people who work like that, but it's not me. It's like being in the densest muddle, fog and undergrowth until you get a glint of something somewhere and you say, "That looks like the end of the forest." When you get there it might only be a clearing but you sit down and make a cup of tea, muster your forces together, then move again. To choose the play in the first place is a hazardous decision. When you read it there's got to be something in you that says, "I think that out of the thickets I can get to daylight." You don't have any idea how, but you'd quite like to go through the process at whatever cost and see how it works. There are other plays — which to somebody else's view may have great theatrical virtues, human virtues, commercial virtues, but I can't for myself see my way through, so I've honestly got to say no. It doesn't dismay me when I see a play I said no to being a wild success, because it was right for that other fellow to do it but not for me.'

He has his own method of working with designers, too. 'I've worked with Voytek a lot, he did *Much Ado* and *Voyage Round My Father* and *Veterans,* and what I like about him is that he's good with the big ideas. He's good at executing them too. There's a danger when the designer sees himself only as an artificer who comes in at a certain point and exits at a certain point. Whereas Voytek takes it upon himself to tell you how you should be directing the actors, how you should be lighting it, what the philosophical implications of the play are, and will bounce around any area quite freely. Some people might not like that if all they want is to be serviced. If you hire a designer like a plumber, then Voytek would be terrible because he'd come in and re-do your shelves but your tap would still be leaking; but he's given me a lot of vigorous insights which I like.

'I'm not very good with the designer who expects me to know all the answers. I need an ally to work out how something should be approached, and it gives me confidence when I know that someone will argue back. It's not good otherwise, because if I work with a designer who is terribly compliant I find myself saying things like, "This play should take place entirely on a traffic island," and if he doesn't flinch but goes away to design a traffic island then I tend, in a suicidal way, to feel, "Oh, well, let's go ahead and do it." We don't, of course. But you do tend to spend emotion and energy — it's not economical in terms of time or money.'

When it comes to earning a living I wondered how he felt about working in the subsidized theatre and Shaftesbury Avenue, and which he preferred or found most difficult. 'The good thing about Shaftesbury Avenue is that if you've got something that works, then it pays well. Don't let anybody kid you — it's quite nice if you have something that actually works to get some financial reward out of it, but, having said that, it can be so troublesome. Shaftesbury Avenue sometimes looks like the worst end of Anglicanism where we put on our best clothes and we go to it and we listen with half an ear and we slip our chocolates along the row, whereas I went to Sheffield the other week where there is this marvellous repertory theatre and I sat through two shows. You know, when a person is present, half present, or not there at all — well, at Sheffield the audience were really present, and they listened and wanted it to happen and were enthusiastic and had a good time.

'It was really special, and you don't get that in Shaftesbury Avenue often. And I hate the trendiness. I went to a show recently which was very much lauded where the audience were acting the notices — it was a hollow response. The things that I've really been excited by have been, as I said, the Theatre Upstairs, the first visit of the French circus at The Round House — these were crucial, merry events, where the response of the audience, whether it likes or resists what it's seeing, isn't dutiful.

'I don't feel cushioned in the subsidized theatre at all. I don't feel cushioned in any theatre. Whether I'm doing a play at Stratford or in the West End I'm in exactly the same hole, and each time there's no guarantee of climbing out of it.'

# Patrick Garland

Patrick Garland describes himself as a natural freelance, and he directs in the subsidized and commercial theatre, and in television, where he also appears from time to time as an interviewer. Although I knew he had been an actor, I somehow assumed that he had always intended to direct, and asked him if this was so.

'By no means. Most people, I suppose, start directing at school, even before that I wouldn't be surprised if they had been directing with enthusiasm what Noël Coward called "those cardboard monstrosities" — that is, little toy theatres. I'm not particularly a believer in fortune-telling from the stars or prognostications from the palms of the hands, but it is a fact that on a number of occasions I have been told that, according to my hand, at one point in my life I would have a complete change of career.

'Anyway, whatever the reason, it is a fact that at the age of about twenty-three I did change. Before that I had never given directing a thought. I'd done some amateur acting both at school and in the Army, but it seems indisputable from recent examples that most directors were deeply involved in directing by the time they were at University, but I certainly was not.

'I was much more interested in writing, and this still remains a very important aspect of my work, and something to which I'd like to return. My involvement in writing went on right through my early education and my years at Oxford. And I still do write — but not enough, to my own discontent. I published poetry from the age of sixteen in *The London Magazine* and the PEN anthology.

'I was lucky in finding, when I was at school, that I was better at acting than most of my contemporaries. I was lucky too because I had very enthusiastic parents who were both of them interested in the arts and were aware of the elements

which could go to help me. I moved to Southampton as a
child — I lived there around the same time as Ken Russell,
in fact — and my parents thought I should widen my activities
beyond the cricket pitch, and duly took me to see concerts,
plays, ballets, foreign films, and they also encouraged me to
join an amateur dramatic society which turned out to be one
of the best in the country. It had a very great influence on
me and it sent me up to Oxford University equipped to act
in OUDS productions, as I had a tremendous amount of
valuable experience, and I didn't have to go having played
Viola in *Twelfth Night* or having read only *Macbeth* in the
sixth form.

'In fact, this society was several times a finalist in the
British Drama League Festivals, in spite of the fact that
Southampton was a complete cultural desert — but it urged
me to get out, no bad thing. I think probably the drama
director of that Society, a man called Rodney Spratley, was
one of the biggest influences on me. He taught me what it
was to "direct", not just to put plays on but how to interpret
them, work them out and express them, even though I was
only acting in them at the time and wasn't interested in
directing.'

At this point I mentioned that everyone I'd spoken to of
about our age had directed away like mad in the Army, and
that I could imagine the country covered in little tented
camps where would-be directors enthusiastically put on
concert parties and one-act plays, in ignorance of each other's
activities.

'Yes, I did go into the Army, which dates all of us who did
National Service. Years later, I met Sir John Gielgud and he
asked me about Robin Phillips. He said, "I believe he's a very
talented man; he really knows his stuff, and he's quite young,
isn't he?" And I said, "Yes, he is very young, in fact we were
both actors at the Bristol Old Vic together." "Oh, then he's
not *so* young," said Sir John, making one of his celebrated
gaffes. Anyway, off I went to do my National Service, and I
suppose you can say I got quite decent parts in play-readings,
though that's hardly what everybody goes into the Royal
Artillery for. I never got a commission. I was stationed at
Southend-on-Sea and spent quite a lot of spare time working

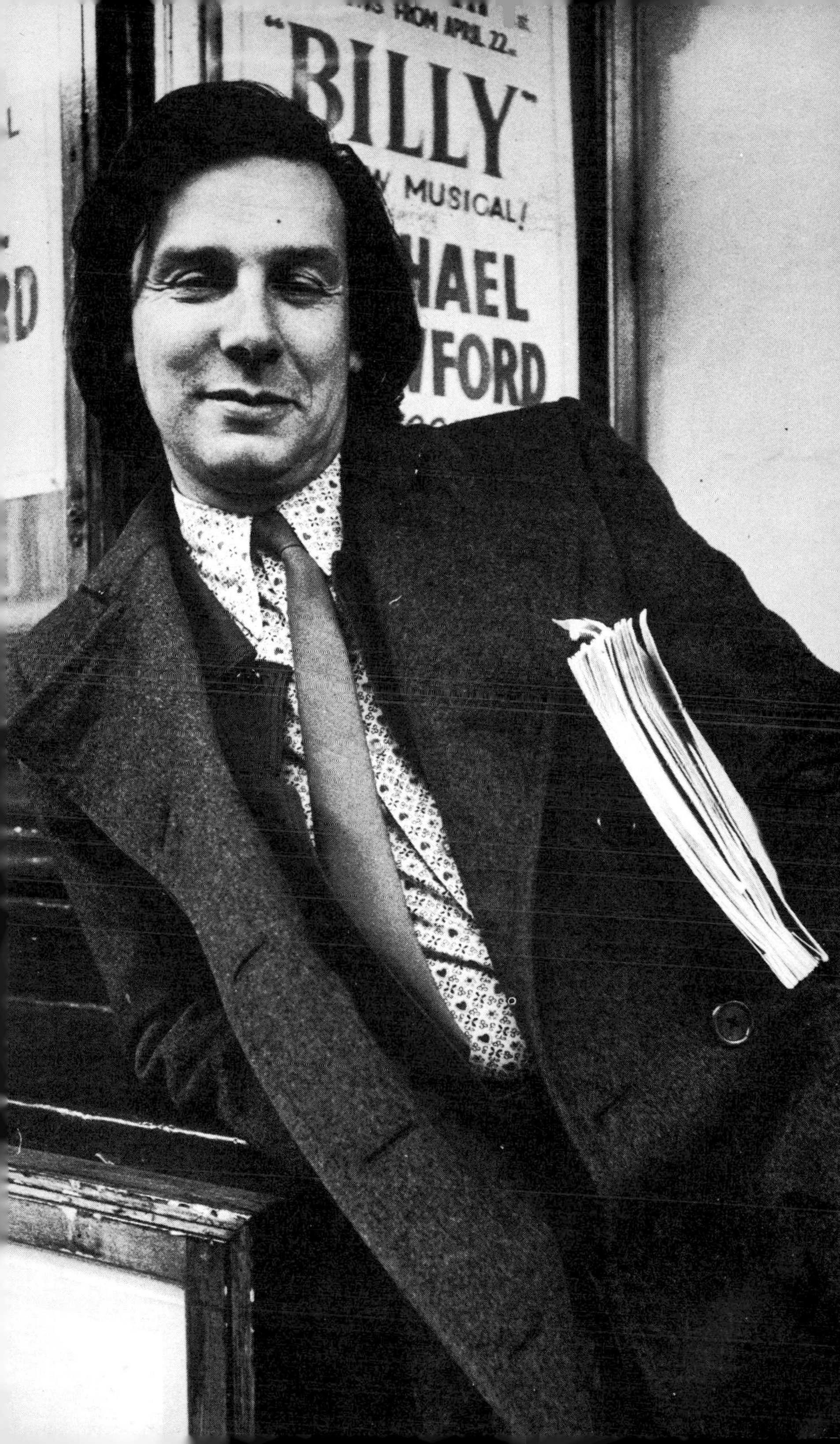


Photo: PETER HOWE

in the fairgrounds there. It was better than being a one-pip. Because of my experiences working in the Kursaal in my hours off, as well as writing short stories, I wrote a couple of plays, and they were produced later on television. My Commanding Officer then told me in order to become an officer I should try and do something useful for the regiment like athletics, and in those days I was quite a good athlete, so I ended up a regimental athlete and — although this is almost impossible to believe — a regimental boxer. I also acted as a sort of "feed" to the officers' wives in the Regimental Play-Reading Society — John Stride was my troop commander.

'But there was a flaw in all this. When I'd finally achieved my aims in eight months, after trying really hard, my Commanding Officer ordered me in again and said, "Garland, now you've become a regimental athlete and boxer, and you're indispensable to the Dramatic Society, we can't possibly give you a commission so you'll have to stay here." So I spent my entire time at Southend. Mud Island, they called it! You could call me, I suppose, a cultivated Bombardier. One incident will always stay with me. There was a big regimental parade in front of about two thousand people, and after a long period of waiting one of the O.R.'s said loudly without his lips moving, "They also serve who only stand and wait." One peculiarly thick sergeant slammed his heels together and yelled out, "Who said *that?*" and the soldier replied — with a certain amount of wit, I thought — "Milton, sir!" The sergeant yelled, "Milton — stand out!"'

'Most of my contemporaries, as I said, after school and National Service went on to direct at university, but when I was at Oxford I had no desire to, in fact I had quite a strong disinclination towards directing. If I was interested in anything outside acting plays, it was writing them. But I did have a great success acting, playing leading roles in some very interesting and exciting Oxford productions. I worked for some well-known directors like Peter Dews, for whom I played Henry V, and Anthony Page, for whom I played Coriolanus. I made my debut in *Ghosts* for my College, St Edmund Hall, which was directed by a young undergraduate called John Cox, who was just out of the Navy — and hardly likely to have imagined himself, at that time, Artistic Director at Glyndebourne. I had

a very good and much admired agent and he found me an
audition for the Bristol Old Vic which I enjoyed, on the
surface, but inevitably I had to revise my vision of myself.
When you're at university, anyone seriously involved is
inevitably a leading actor, but when I left I felt the leading
roles had slipped through my grasp. I lost a lot of, not nerve,
but conceit, and I learned that the theatre was going to be
quite different from what I imagined it was going to be.

'Although you see your life as a series of leading roles, it
very rarely is, and this kind of confrontation all actors are
bound to meet. As a result of this, I changed my entire attitude
from that of an enthusiastic and successful amateur into that
of a persistent and tenacious professional, with a loss of
confidence. There were very fine actors all around me, and I
knew I had little hope of being as good as they were. In fact,
my belief in my acting, and in my need to act, began to
disappear. I say this in criticism of myself, for if I'd been
really committed, a "proper actor", I would have disregarded
this. I carried on for a while, but I felt my acting career was
definitely on the downward path. Not entirely, though, for
my good friend Peter Dews, who's been one of my greatest
helpers and severe critic, persuaded me to film *The Age of
Kings* in some very good roles, and this was a marvellous
experience for me. The last part I played was Malcolm in a
splendid open-air *Macbeth* at Ludlow, and although I feel
occasional nostalgia for acting, it is remote, and not
connected with actually *wanting* to act again.

'Then an event took place which was very important, but of
which I was quite unconscious at the time. Frith Banbury saw
one of my plays on television, *The Hard Case* (which Peter
Wood had directed), and he gave me some money to write him
a play. Then came the crunch, when I had to decide whether
or not to go on acting or start to write. You know, it's one of
those things where you say, "If only I had the money, I know
what I'd spend it on!" and suddenly I did have the money, so
I decided to take the opportunity to give up acting. I went to
Paris, and this was a very necessary period of transition, though
now I wish I'd done a little more time as an actor, even another
year. I think it would have made some difference. I'm glad I
did act, because I think this part of the director's relationship

with an actor as an actor is part of my strength. Actors are always underrated, and their problems misunderstood — they spend most of their lives feeling exposed, and I know that feeling. I'm not a person who believes that the actor is the be-all and end-all of a production. I'm certain it is a combination of the writer, designer and director which makes the most valuable contribution to the pleasure and delight which an actor at his best gives an audience. But they are ultimately the ones who have to *do* it — and on occasion endure it. Actors without plays are poor creatures, but plays without actors are no creatures at all.

'In Paris I lived very cheaply and rather typically in a hotel with a lot of picaresque expatriates, unperturbed really by life in Paris at the time of the Algerian crisis, which somewhat resembled Belfast. "Plastiques" were often going off. In a way, life hadn't changed much there along the rue Mouffetard since the 1920s or even 1890s. That is to say, it was a good experience for an Englishman who had been very conventionally brought up through the Army and university. The result was it upset a very large number of the rather respectable values I'd picked up, and I would like to think it altered irretrievably my attitude towards what things are.'

'Then I was approached by David Jones, who was working on *Monitor,* a programme which was at the height of its fame, and has never been surpassed or successfully imitated, and I received one of those unexpected moments of good fortune in life — and I turned it down! I was offered a job as a research assistant, but there was no doubt that at that time I wanted to write, *was* writing plays and short stories, and I wanted to carry on like that, to live in Paris "on the edge" rather than belong to a large organization like the Royal Shakespeare Company, the Old Vic, BBC or whatever. It just wasn't in my temperament or emotion at the time. I said no, the job went to somebody else, and a whole year went by. Then David wrote to me again and said, "The job's come up once more," and he urged me to consider it most carefully, and this time I did, and I blush when I think about it; it wasn't what I wanted to do. But in the end I did, and that was the beginning of my being a director. So there's a tremendous connection between David and me. If you have any belief in

destiny or what Romans call "fortuna", and I do to a very
highly developed degree, there was a case in point of
opportunity knocking twice.

'*Monitor* had some superb producers working for it,
Humphrey Burton, Ken Russell, John Schlesinger, David
Jones, Nancy Thomas, and my fellow-researcher was Melvyn
Bragg. Most of the inspiration came from Huw Wheldon. He
had a profound enthusiasm and a sense of — for want of a
better term — life values, many of which I think I share. While
working for Wheldon I discovered a growing interest in the
craft of a director, but by chance — not consciously. There
was something inevitable about every Sunday's programme,
and I was meeting some kind of a deadline. I learned to edit
film, or at least to make sense of it, to acquire that instinctive
sense of pace and rhythm, how to shape and construct, tune
to an audience, and most important of all to adopt that
guiding line, that course where you can please both an
audience and yourself, which up until then I'd ignored completely. From there it was a small step to begin directing
things on my own. And I was above all lucky — Melvyn
Bragg and I and about six others in Lime Grove, I always
think, got the last of the wine. The BBC has changed a lot
since those rather halcyon days, when it resembled a benevolent
Bloomsbury.

'But I'm not a person who can work under the umbrella
of a big company very easily. If I had been able to work in
this way I'd have been working for the BBC still. I admire
passionately what they do and their attitude to what they do,
and I had tremendous pleasure out of working there, especially
from the people, with whom I have always remained emotionally close. Perhaps the flaw lies in me, if it is a flaw; it's a
question of temperament, not a good thing or a bad thing,
but just me. Stephen Hearst, then head of BBC Arts, told me
I was a born freelance, and I'm completely reconciled to this.
It's the variety which gives me enjoyment, the West End run,
working with undergraduates, poetry festivals, new plays at
Hampstead, television, all kind of things. I need a fairly lavish
quota of risk in my life — and get it. Security, whether
professional or emotional, makes me curiously insecure.'

I then asked him how he approached a play. 'Almost to a

fault, I can say I'm a very unintellectual and non-analytical person, though I read a great deal and examine things in detail, which should be, I suppose, the attributes of an intellectual person. But I'm not one, and therein lies whatever faults and virtues are contained in that attitude. There are plenty of "thinkers" about, and not all of them are thinking straight. In general I belong to a narrative tradition but I'm rather keen not to be too limited by that. I have learned — not before time, I might say — to explore more experimental non-narrative style, and I learned a lot about that from my experience of directing *Hair* in Israel, where, for the first time ever, I was confronted with working on something which genuinely did not express itself in language, but in images and choreography and in physical shapes. Up to that time I really hadn't believed that was possible. Now I know for a fact that it is.

'I do like plays to mean something, although I'm not stuck with that. One of the most important plays that I've seen recently without *any* doubt at all, without rival or competitor, is Peter Handke's *The Ride Across Lake Constance,* and that would seem to be an example of a piece of work where to sit about and simply say "What is it about?", "What does it mean?", is as futile as to approach music in that way. I wouldn't conceivably approach a piece of chamber music like, say, a Mozart Quintet and say, "It sounds very nice, but what does it mean?" I would hope to assimilate it in a different way.

'But by and large, I do respond to a narrative formal tradition, and I look for plays of eloquence and articulateness. I like good language, where the writer has taken pains not just to write but to write as well as he can, as opposed to what Kingsley Amis rightly describes as the modern law of writing, "Never write a good sentence if a bad sentence will do." I would shrink from that even in the theatre, where you can get away with quite a lot of bad sentences. If the perfect three-act play came along I doubt that I should want to do it. I must be attracted to plays that need work done on them, and with some collaboration from the earliest stage with the author and the actor. In nearly everything I've directed, with the exception of an Ibsen play — and even that had a

translator/adaptor and plays by Shakespeare — I've always
done that.

'I don't like to interfere with plays that are already in their
shape; that doesn't interest me. I hate it when I see people
put Shakespeare's scenes round about. They're nearly always
wrong, they never illuminate and they're dealing in that case
with someone who really did know what he was talking
about. They would have sorted that out in 1608 or whenever
it was.

'I like the spirit of collaboration in the theatre. I think
there are examples when you don't need it; there are writers
who really don't need their second acts rewritten, there are
actors who don't want a director in any other sense but to
take care of the rest of the people, and spend time with them
personally; they're very exceptional actors of enormous
perception and experience. In both cases I regard them as
rarities. Only a few modern plays seem to be complete; many
could be better, and a great many from the subsidized
theatres invariably shorter. Now, it does interest me very
much to work on something which is incomplete with the
author, and which needs the author/director/actor to
complete it. Above all, *Forty Years On* was like this, and
that to me is the most exciting way of working in plays. I'm
still doing it. I believe most strongly in the playwright,
Nicholas Salaman, who has written three plays. He did *Mad
Dog* this summer. It wasn't liked in general by the critics, but
I had a totally different intention in mind, a crusading
purpose if you like, and felt very firmly that until a writer
gets his first play on he can't begin to know what the theatre
is made of. We achieved that, and it was a classic example of
an author who was greatly encouraged by seeing his play on
after three years struggle and disappointment. First plays by
even the greatest dramatists are seldom perfect — not even
Shakespeare's, Chekhov's, Ibsen's and Strindberg's.

'Adverse criticism is something you just have to take in
your stride. Nobody gets bouquets all the time, even though
I fear that's what one subconsciously craves for — it worries
me sometimes when I see somebody shot down with a whole
barrage of artillery when a single pistol shot would have done.
Some criticism is spiteful and envious, and of late worryingly

eccentric; sometimes the critics are wrong, sometimes you are. When Salaman's new play is finished, then we'll see if the whole experiment was worthwhile. And I shall reserve a special basilisk glare for the yahoo critics in the audience who lacked perception.

'Turning once more to the actor, I think there's a moment when every new production changes, when it ceases to be composed of the characters in the author's and director's mind, when it becomes the living people you've got there on the stage. That happens after about two and a half weeks of rehearsal. That is the crucial area where a director plays a very important role, where you face the reality of the theatre and what the audience is going to see. The audience is no longer able to know or even discern what was earlier in your mind, nor would they be interested. It's no good saying, "Look, in the character of George instead of *this actor*, you should be seeing someone who is five years younger, has blond hair, etc." — that's of no interest at all. This can be a great area of conflict between writer and director — when an actor is being asked to do something he is incapable of doing because you've cast him wrongly, or where he is interpreting a character wrongly from the author's point of view.

'I think tact is very important. I sometimes have an inhibition that too much of my energy is devoted to tact and diplomacy, like certain politicians; you're so busy being diplomatic you don't achieve anything. I think it's just a little human sensitivity that is needed, and the reverse of that, which I dread, is insensitivity. Personally, I'm very easily crushed by anyone who comes racing in, and treads all over me. It isn't difficult for them to do it; the only effect is to crush me, it doesn't make me any different, merely crushed. I'm neither influenced particularly, nor affected, but I just don't bother to express an opinion. I feel like that about actors; they're generally very vulnerable and sensitive. There are ways of saying things and getting through to people. Actors over-directed, or strait-jacketed, are frequently more negative than when left alone to themselves. That's where casting is so vital.

'My friend Roy Dotrice, with whom I have this splendid relationship over the creation of *Brief Lives,* which is a

collaboration in the very best sense — in fact, we often laugh
over the fact that we can't any more discover where one left
off and the other began — pulls my leg and tells me when I
say, "It may be my impression, I may be wrong, but the other
night when I came to see the play, well, the audience enjoyed
it, and yes, it did go well, I suppose, and maybe I came on a
bad night, but it did occur to me that one moment in the
second act, etc. . . . " I really mean, it's blindingly dreadful.
People can laugh, and I realize I'm a bit circuitous, but it's
only my kind of personal language, and anyone working with
me for long knows what I'm trying to say. I've never been
the least bit impressed by people who pride themselves on
telling you outright what they think. Candour is a rather
unlikeable moral virtue.

'I think everybody working in the arts looks back on their
experiences, with certain mountain peaks to enjoy — and
indeed, conversely, deep chasms to regret — and there's no
doubt in my mind that I have two tremendously joyful
experiences, both of which without any doubt at all
utterly affected my career, and hence my life — they were
the productions of *Forty Years On* and *Brief Lives. Brief
Lives* existed in a shape before *Forty Years On,* but with
regard to the actual influence on my professional career, it
was the success of *Forty Years On* which happened first in
the West End, by two or three months, and it was the first
time I'd worked with Sir John Gielgud; a privilege for an
untried director. It wasn't the start of my collaboration with
Alan Bennett, but it was part of our history. We knew each
other at Oxford, where he had acquired a great reputation
for doing underground cabaret (I do mean literally "under
the ground", as he acted in College cellars!) but he was a very,
very private person. He still is.

'We saw each other from time to time, and I can claim some
tiny credit for having wooed him fractionally towards the
theatre, though he's not a person who can be wooed or
influenced very much. When I was working in the BBC he sent
me some scripts which later became his series *On the Margin*
for which he deservedly won the Comedy Award of the Year;
and also, as I was doing my own series of *Famous Gossips,*
which began with Roy Dotrice as John Aubrey, I directed

Alan in one, in which he played the Victorian Augustus Hare. After that he sent me the first mass of material which later became *Forty Years On,* but was then called *The Last of England,* and of course it enjoyed a prodigious success. It didn't, may I say, when we opened in Manchester, and Alan has written about that much better than I do — he kept a journal. But after a half-hearted beginning, we got into our stride at Brighton and it became a great success. Above all it was an enormously *happy* time. I don't think it's possible for me to look back on a happier time than those months, because all of us had achieved so much in an innocent way, without intending to. Alan received a gigantic response to his first play, and so had I — I'd really never produced at all — we neither of us knew what that kind of success was going to be like. It was just immensely pleasurable. We loved the company of the boys, who were endlessly refreshing, and badly behaved, and comical and enchanting. It's extraordinary to think they're all in their middle twenties now. Even the Rolling Stones are in their thirties! Over all this was our immense joy in working with John Gielgud, and the thrill of creating together a genuinely original comic play. For what it's worth, and at the risk of seeming arrogant, I do rate the play very highly, and I think of it in the very exalted terms that Bernard Levin wrote of it in his book on the Sixties. I look back with nostalgia to a haunting experience that will never be repeated.

'I also picked up the taste for Shaftesbury Avenue, the particular tang and tension of London's real theatrical life. For all its faults, and it is unprotected, and rapacious, and has a short memory — it is bluntly exposed in a way, emphatically, the subsidized theatre is not. You have to succeed with a general audience — three hundred times a year — the support of the intelligentsia, the underground, the cultured middle-class, the newspaper critics is not enough. It is nonsense to assume you cannot be first-rate and intensely popular — although the combination is desparately hard to achieve.

'The entire event of *Forty Years On* was tremendously significant and thrilling for me in actual personal terms of enjoying something I'd worked on — which generally I don't do. I feel very objective about it. I feel the piece belongs to the actors somehow, and I sit in the stalls on an opening night feeling rather forlorn and left out. There are two occasions when I didn't, *Twelfth Night,* which I directed at Oxford last year with undergraduates, and the best of all, Roy Dotrice in *Brief Lives.* I never felt I wrote *Brief Lives,* I felt in an unsentimental way — and so did Roy Dotrice — that the spirit of John Aubrey hovered over it. But it was a very intricate and complicated piece of theatre. There were moments when Roy was performing before an audience which was not only enjoying it, and being entertained, but was *absolutely spell-bound,* captivated to a most remarkable degree. Some of the most exhilarating moments I've ever known took place in that production. Hard to explain, simply shared moments. We did it very much in a spirit of collaboration, to let Roy express and explore this remarkable old character and for me to have a shot at seeing if I could hold the stage with a play for one man. We expected it would have a run of about three distinguished weeks at Hampstead — we never expected more than that, and it's still popular.

'I feel very warmly about actors, and have had the very closest and happiest relationships with those I've worked with — with the exception of a very, very few. I'm conceited enough to enjoy — and I make no secret of it — the fact that in almost every production which has worked well either the actor or author has received an award. Alan Bennett got the TV Comedy award for *On the Margin,* Roy Dotrice won two awards, for stage and television, John Gielgud won the Evening Standard Actor of the Year award, and Alan Bennett again won an award for *Forty Years On* and *Getting On* for the best comedy of the year. Claire Bloom won a firm award for *A Doll's House,* Jenny Agutter won an Emmy for *The Snow Goose.* Those distinctions mean a great deal to me. Best Director's Award doesn't, because I like to take a back seat, I like it to seem as unnoticeable as possible. I like an audience to feel the actors are totally in command, that they've made a kind of benevolent putsch. Fussy direction annoys me. I don't respond to intrusive direction in either a film or a play, and the directors I admire are reticent ones, although I respect Brook as a great innovator. When the curtain goes up I like to feel that enormous reticent authority: the actor is sitting on that chair for twenty minutes because he wants to. There's no uncertainty about it, no hesitation.

'The intrusion of the director can best be described by what Lord David Cecil, who was my tutor, once said to a friend of mine who had written a flashy essay on Jacobean theatre: "There's nothing wrong with it at all, it's terribly good, it's very erudite, and well composed, but if you insist on my saying something critical, I do find it relentlessly bright!" I do take great care and pains about my response to an actor in a play because that's what plays are all about. It always comes back in the end to the fact that they are the ones who have to do it. Acting is very difficult, and infinitely harder than it looks. It's harder than singing and dancing. When you work with good actors, as I do nine-tenths of the time, you find yourself thinking acting is very easy, but it's a most complicated mechanism; it's much easier to play the piano very well. You practise and practise, and if you're good you go to a concert hall and *play,* but acting isn't only practice and talent, there's a terrible exposure of self. All human beings surround themselves with layers of protection to prevent exposure, and yet actors are in part required and impelled to reveal themselves all the time. If you can in any way aid and abet that process as a director, then it's both a privilege and a delight.

'I feel when I am working on any production that I am privileged to take part, for a small moment in time, in a community. I have a distinct social sense of the company I am with, from the most affluent producer to the most modest apprentice stage-manager. I also have this deep-rooted feeling that a great deal of what goes into a production, into the result of the many people involved in a play, will spread into the audience. Not all the time, admittedly. There are countless examples of companies which dislike each other intensely, and plays that go through the most unimaginably difficult birth-pangs, which turn into great successes. Much more sadly, there are devoted companies whose rehearsal-periods have been an uninterrupted love affair, where all the omens are favourable, that turn out utter disasters. I still persist in believing that some of the affection that goes into making a work of theatre (to say nothing of the frustration, complication and downright boredom) will permeate the audience that watches it.

'In conclusion, my own feeling when working in the theatre, the satisfaction that it gives me, is also what I feel about the art of writing or of painting. It has everything to do with Reality. Like the celebrated line from one of Wystan Auden's most personal poems; I agree: "Me — alienated? Bosh! It's simply that I feel Most at Home with what is real." Not realism, not naturalism, but those aspects of reality in life which can be captured in art and recognized by other people. I can only put into plays, not what I learnt at school or from technique, but what I have learned personally out of life, what thrills me and moves me. When the theatre divorces itself from reality and turns into an abstraction I'm certainly not saying that it doesn't have great merit, beauty or value, but I am saying that I cannot follow it there, or contribute to it. If I were a writer — which I would like to be — these are the books that I would wish to write: books with a story, character, humour, beginnings, middles and ends; not books about aesthetics or books whose only audience is other writers. The only development that I could possibly see in my work would simply be how my own life develops, and as my life so far has not lacked theatricality, I do not see why it should suddenly dry up or grind to a halt. Auden's poetry has meant more to me than any other modern poet — unless it's Philip Larkin — and Auden saw himself as a poet of disenchantment. In a similar way it is the function of a director to face reality, to be thoroughly disillusioned, but to persist in his hopes, and peddle illusions. I spoke of Auden before because eight short lines of his poem for a child's birthday *Many Happy Returns* expresses everything I feel about things infinitely better than the six hundred lines I've just spoken!

> So I wish you first a
> Sense of theatre; only
> Those who love illusion
>    And know it will go far:
> Otherwise we spend our
> Lives in a confusion
> Of what we say and do with
>    Who we really are.

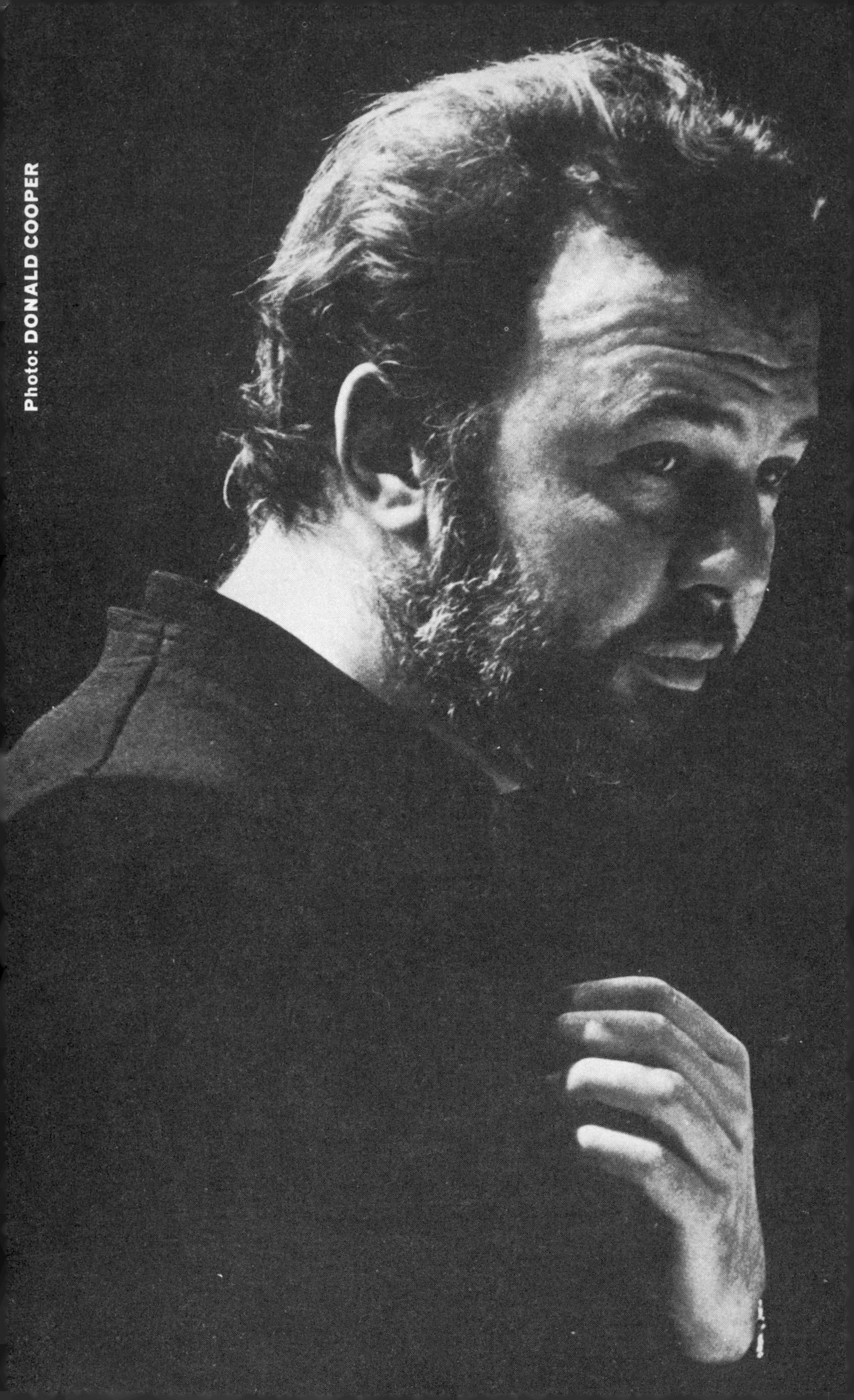

Photo: DONALD COOPER

# Peter Hall

Peter Hall, now director of the National Theatre, has pulled
off a remarkable theatrical hat-trick, having been director of
all three massive State-subsidized companies, the Royal
Shakespeare Company, the Royal Opera Company, and now
the National. His years at Stratford produced a real sense of
style as well as a revolution in the way Shakespeare was
presented by the company which owes its existence to him.
Whether or not the RSC really produced an ensemble
company in the true sense of the word is open to a variety of
interpretations, but certainly under Peter Hall's directorship,
as later under that of Trevor Nunn, the RSC became a
cohesive unit.

He was one of the few directors who knew what he wanted
to do from a very early age. 'It was a combination of
ignorance and instinct, equally compounded. I was very stage-
struck, and liked going to the theatre at an early age. I was
very interested in acting, in music and in design, but I never
wanted to be an actor. I discovered fairly early on that there
was somebody behind the scenes who was in some sense
responsible for all this happening, so I wanted to be a director
when I was fourteen. I don't mean I knew what being a
director *was* at fourteen, but I remember I read quite a lot
about Craig when I was about fifteen or sixteen. I read all his
published work, and there was a book towards the end of the
war, or a little after, called *The Other Theatre*, by Norman
Marshall, which was about art theatre in England in the
thirties, and that absolutely fascinated me. To anyone who
is stage-struck descriptions of theatre past always sound
marvellous.

'Then I got into reading about Stanislavsky and went to an
awful lot of theatre. I saw Peter Brook's first production at
Stratford, which was marvellous, absolutely shattering; I was
also very jealous because he was only twenty or twenty-one

at the time and I was still at school. I saw all the Gielgud
seasons at the Haymarket, the Olivier/Richardson seasons at
the New, and I grew up in the war years in Cambridge, where
there was a great deal of theatre because of the wartime
conditions; and also good amateur theatre, mainly the
Marlowe Society.

   'My National Service I spent in Germany. I was very
impressed, because although they had very little food and
very little money, the theatre, as a subsidized part of the
community's life, was still operating. I was near Hanover, and
the Opera House was functioning in the stables of the old
Elector of Hanover's Palace. That was the first time I saw
*Tristan.* I think everything conspired to make me try to find
out what a director was.

   'I had absolutely no idea whether I could be a director — I
shouldn't think any of us ever have. How could we? And
there's no way of training to be one either, which I think is
regrettable. Most of my generation became directors by
having sufficient *chutzpah* (there's no English word for it) to
say in our early twenties, "I'm a director." If we said it with
sufficient *chutzpah* we were believed sometimes, and we
directed plays. We became directors by directing. I think
that's an awful waste of other people's talent, the people who
are working with you, and a pretty crucifying experience for
yourself.

   'I was a teacher in the RAF. I taught economics and
business management, which is pretty unbelievable in a way,
but I've always been interested in administration and finance.
There is a side of a director which is partly administrative. If
a director doesn't choose priorities, he never gets a play on.
Although some directors might hotly contest the fact that
they are partly pragmatists, I think they have to be.

   'While you're in a situation where you can say, "Nobody
has said no to being in my play," you can, in your mind's
eye, cast it with the world. But once you have your actors,
once they are engaged, you have to do your work with them
and use what you have. That is in some sense management.
You can't be creative in the theatre without having a
management sense. An actor has to have a sense of management towards himself — learning how to pace himself.

'You asked me why I wanted to be a director? Through
academic training, I had a very strong leaning towards words,
I mean plays and books. Equally, I was fascinated from my
teens on with sociology and the community and economics.
I was made into an academic by the scholarship rat-race,
which I suspect was a little more rigorous then than it is
now. As far as my college was concerned, I was supposed to
be an academic, not a theatre person. I thought if I didn't
make it in the theatre, I could always be a teacher. Though
I didn't want to teach.

'I've always had the feeling that the coming together of
the audience and the performer is one of the few opportunities
in our society for a debate in live terms. What's done on the
stage affects those who do it. You don't get that in any other
media. It is that quality of the theatre which, as well as
being partly for enjoyment, is part a church and part a
political meeting that fascinated me and that has remained
(though obviously I've changed from year to year). But that's
very basic. There are few things to me more marvellous than
an audience which is actually being lit by a theatre experience.
It doesn't even have to be a very good piece of theatre. But
it's an extraordinary thing to observe.

'It's marvellously satisfying. To sit among an audience that's
applauding because they absolutely want to, I find an extraordinary experience. Laughter is the same, when an audience is
made helpless with laughter. The sort of feeling there is in
*Saturday, Sunday, Monday;* the craft of the playwright
releases such a feeling of joy and happiness in the audience
that you can hardly believe it. It's amazing.

'When I'm working on a production the first reaction is
instinctive. Do I want to do the play at this moment? I cannot
possibly rationalize that instinct. There are plays that you
read that you want to do at a certain moment; plays that you
don't want to do at that time; plays you think are worth
seeing but that you don't want to do. It's an instinctive
reaction on the first reading. If you have an instinct that you
want to do it, it's like an actor wanting to play a part. You
can rationalize why you have that instinctive reaction later.
Those rationalizations may or may not be true. It's like saying
to a writer, "Why did you write that rather than that?" It's

the observers of one's work who trace patterns and obsessions.
But I think if we are aware of them ourselves we become
terribly self-conscious, trendy and cunning. And un-instinctive.

'I'm now directing a Shakespeare play for the first time in
six years. I've directed twenty-four of the plays, and have been
away from Shakespeare for six years deliberately. Shakespeare
had been the centre of my life academically and theatrically
from the time I was twelve or thirteen. Six years ago I thought
it was time to stop for a rest. Now I'm coming back to do a
play — *The Tempest* — that I've always wanted to do and
never dared to do. I hardly dare do it now, but the need to
do it is very strong, and it links up in me with a feeling that
it's about the nature of art and the artist — the need for and
yet the pointlessness of art. I think it's a very bleak play. Here
is a man who could invent an infinite number of magic visions
and images in order to order harsh reality. Yet he stops at the
end and says, "What is the point in doing it anyway?" He
hasn't changed man's nature one whit by making all those
shapes. He hasn't changed anything. I find that a very penetra-
ting analysis of the artist in society. He has to do it, but once
he's done it, it all has to be done again. He makes nothing that
is final.

'On a technical level I want to do *The Tempest* because
I've become very interested in emblematic theatre. And that
has led me to the meaning of the baroque theatre, the baroque
opera, the masque and the theatre of Inigo Jones. I think we
are perhaps a little puritanical as a nation about the visual
theatre. We are apt to think that as soon as Inigo Jones came
into the Jacobean theatre, the writer was driven out. I don't
believe that. The emblematic, visual side of the theatre — if
you have a great artist doing it — is immensely potent. *The
Tempest* is about that. It's the old man writing a play using
the new fashion, using the new technique of the masque. All
this is much in my mind at the moment — which is an added
reason why I want to do *The Tempest*.'

*The Tempest* has obviously fascinated him for years, and
when I talked to him three years ago he said then that it was
what he most wanted to do, adding, 'For me, the real crux
of the play is at the end where Miranda says "O brave new
world, that has such people in't!" and Prospero says, " 'Tis new

to thee." Every generation is disillusioned, and is replaced
by a hopeful generation.

'It's been with me ever since I left Stratford but the time
has never seemed right. There isn't another Shakespeare play
I want to do at this moment, but once I've done *The Tempest*
I hope I'll want to do another.

'I don't believe you can do a play unless you can say as a
director what you think the spine of it is. It is about many
things, of course — but you must know what its centre is to
you. I'm not sure you should say what it is to your cast, and
I'm pretty certain you shouldn't say it to the public or the
Press, but you have to know it yourself. What it means to
you. It has to come out of a knowledge of the text which, if
you're working well, contains in Shakespeare's case a fraction
of his metaphor — which is why I can tell you what *The
Tempest* is to me. One has to read the play over and over and
over again so that you actually know it in your blood.

'There are two different aspects to a director's work. In a
modern play, his job is to stimulate modern signals of
behaviour, and reflections of that behaviour which his
contemporary has written. That's difficult, but not all that
difficult, because your language is the same and what we
mean by our signals (our social clubs, our inflections, our
expressions) is the same. From age to age, people's looks
actually change, the way they make up, the way they do
their hair; and the language of social communication changes
from decade to decade. If you hear a record of somebody
speaking in 1930 their accent has an entirely different quality.
It's born of a different society, a different way of life — there
are a myriad things that change. So, the signals we send to
each other about social behaviour change.

'A director's task is to stimulate those signals and edit them
so that the play lives. In a modern play it's fairly straight-
forward. But in an old play, where the signals are different
and are not being made to a society which has the same
receivers, the problems are more complex. You have to know
what Shakespeare's signals are, and then think of a way of
getting them through to a modern audience. That's why I
think that doing Shakespeare in modern dress is on the whole
crazy (because though it illuminates much, it always cuts off

much). It is a direct and crude way of making *some* signals
operate. Perhaps the logical step then is that you rewrite the
text and make it modern. Ultimately, I see nothing wrong in
that in principle. It's what translations do all the time. And
by doing it you are not destroying Shakespeare's works:
they still exist. Fortunately, though, Shakespeare doesn't
*need* rewriting yet. But he might in two hundred years,
when his signals are carefully obscured.

'To interpret and edit these signals when dealing with a
classical text requires an enormous amount of study, so that
you know the social background. You know the society the
play was written for, and approximately how they would
have received it; what it was about, how it was dressed, what
the words actually meant then, as opposed to what they
mean now. Many words have changed their meaning in
Shakespeare, for instance. So the element of scholarship is
important. You have to speak from a knowledge that you
wear lightly.

'The first step in creating a production is the design. No
conception of a play can surmount a wrong design, or a design
that's not clear or that doesn't mean anything. Unfortunately,
the way our theatre's organized, you often have to design a
play before you've found the spine of it. I think you ought to
find it with the actors and then design it halfway through the
finding — the rehearsals. I try and work with a designer with
as many options open as possible. When we actually come to
rehearse we can use the set in slightly different ways. It's
mobile to some extent.

'Rehearsals fall into two very different parts. The first is
very free and very open. You try anything that occurs to
anybody in order to find the life of the play. You find the
richest possible pattern of signals. Second, during the last ten
days, the director's function is editorial and technical, when
you edit all those signals and discard a lot of them. This is
where you have to apply the test "That's very nice, but is it
necessary?" The company may be doing many things they
love that are illustrative, or to use Brecht's term, culinary.
Not actual. The editing is a different gear that you have to
switch into. The first person to be ruthless with is yourself;
if you're going to be ruthless to other people, you have to

be the same to yourself. That's where technique comes in. But it is only the servant of creativity in the actor or the director.

'I imagine the way I've worked has changed over the last few years, though I'm not very aware of it. I think I've become more open to experiment in the first stage and more meticulous in the second. Two extremes. I always used to start at Stratford with a talk to the cast. I thought we ought to share as much background knowledge to the play as could be encapsulated in an hour's talk. Now I think that perhaps a better way of working in the early stages is to read the play innumerable times with the cast, breaking off to discuss it and open up as you go along.'

How does he envisage the National Theatre? 'I think it has to be — for me anyway — cohesive. That isn't to say there can't be a National Theatre which isn't cohesive. But for me the style of a theatre comes out of a group of people working together at a certain place and time and to a certain audience. It's not something that is premeditated or calculated; it happens. People actually need to work together. If everybody is coming and going, that particular cohesion doesn't happen, and although you may do very fine work, the failures don't lead to success. It's not a continuing productive progress.

'I have different feelings now to those I had in 1958-9 when I took over Stratford. I have a stronger feeling about the theatre as a community within the community. I'm less interested now in the feeling that the world's classics must be made widely available. In large measure, this has been done. You can now see up and down the country an enormous number of plays that used to be extremely rare. That was certainly not true fifteen years ago. I think the principle of an ensemble of people who work together has been proved to be one means of running a theatre. Of course, I haven't got a house dramatist here, I haven't got Shakespeare. Given the amount of Shakespeare's work I've done in the past, I find that change a blessing.

'I think it's a very interesting moment in our theatre. I think the time is ripe for a new impulse. If the commercial theatre isn't renewed, it may die. And the big revolution of the English theatre which began underground in the fifties and surfaced with George Devine and the Royal Court, the coming of Sam Beckett, Ionesco and Pinter, the RSC, the National and all the regional subsidized theatres (followed by the reaction against institutions which occurred in the mid-sixties with the fringe) has spent itself. Both the institutions and the fringe have come to the end of a period. Perhaps the institutions should de-institutionalize themselves and the fringe institutionalize — at least to some degree. As usual it's all contradictions and paradoxes. But it's wide open to new approaches.

'Perhaps in some ways the English theatre is a little smug. We've been told by so many people for so many years that we have the best theatre in the world that we're in danger of believing it. Because of what happened in the fifties we have a band of writers we couldn't have hoped for in 1954. Twenty years ago, though you could see Shakespeare, it was difficult to find performances of the rest of the world repertoire, or new plays by British authors. All that has changed. The revolution of increased subsidy through the Arts Council sent our theatres surging ahead in the 1960s, and the number of people going to the serious theatre has grown.

'But any theatre must always seek to widen its audience. The audience must be regarded as part of the effort, part of the art. An alive theatre has an audience drawn from the whole of society. An exclusive social class, whether upper or lower, young or old, makes for a bad audience. A static audience has the potential to transfer its immobility to the product itself.

'In the new South Bank building we've got the best theatre instrument I've ever seen anywhere in the world. It's a quite amazing place. If the National Theatre Company can take the building and master it and not allow it to run *us* (for I don't think buildings make theatre; they're just hellishly useful adjuncts to the work), then we should be all right. It must be a place for the community, meaning London in the small sense, and the nation in the broad sense. It should be a centre in the middle of London where we can be in hourly touch with our audience in all kinds of ways.

'The doors must be open all day to the fringe, to musicians, to poets, to the young with their experiments, from here or the other side of the world; not in the interests of compre-

hensiveness or trendiness, but because this is one small way
to keep the theatre alive. It must in a very real sense be the
nation's theatre. In our studio, I hope it will be possible for
writers to experiment with ideas, and, if they come off, end
up running side by side with *Lear* in the main house.'

I asked him what his policy would be about taking the
National out on tour. I will always remember a tired and
cynical RSC actor who had just done a grilling Theatregoround tour, while also working in the main house,
commenting on the news that the National was going to do a
mini tour: "Well, once they get to Watford they'll need scouts,
because the National have no idea what the rest of the country's
like." ' Peter Hall is well aware that there is a lot of criticism of
the National's touring record.

'We're going to try to tour for about twelve weeks a year
with the main productions and for many more with the
Mobiles. But I don't think it will work unless the regional
theatres come to us as well. There must be that kind of
diversity. We want the regional theatres to come and play on
the South Bank.

'You must always disturb people when your theatre is alive,
because art always challenges preconceptions. As a nation we
are usually sceptical of dogma, whatever its political com-
plexion. So the need to ask questions in our theatre is strong.
It's a small part of democracy. But the other side of national
scepticism is national cosiness. If something works we're
inclined to let it go on working. Actors and audiences tend
towards the comfort of what they have always done or seen,
although they will readily admit that they only feel alive in
the playhouse when convention is challenged. It may then
either be contradicted or endorsed. It's like falling in love;
it's dangerous and disquieting, but a true experience that
everyone seeks.

'I wouldn't dare say that my tastes are or should be other
people's. But I think you can only follow your own tastes.
Otherwise the public don't follow the theatre. If you do plays
in the interest of comprehensiveness, and not because you
passionately want to do them, the public are not interested.
I'm trying here — with this extraordinary group of people
that I've collected around me — to have my own prejudices

challenged as much as possible while reserving the right to follow them.

'Working in the theatre is a quest. What we find today must be discarded tomorrow before we depend on it unthinkingly. That isn't comfortable, but our direct contact with our audience is our reward; direct communication with a community. Is that naive? I will let it stand because it's the nearest I can get to a definition of the theatre. When theatre and audience truly speak to each other, it's a very extraordinary thing. It is beyond human reason, and it is why we work in, or go to, the theatre.

'It's difficult to assess what you've done but I was talking to William Gaskill the other day and he said, "Well, we're none of us young any more, but at least, *we're still here*." That's something, I suppose. Then I wonder — what next? It's a question that always needs asking in the theatre.'

# David Jones

David Jones is a director of great sensitivity, whether he is
dealing with the struggling downtrodden remnants of people
in *The Lower Depths* or with the complicated ritual game of
love in *Love's Labour's Lost*. His work is neither revolution-
ary nor flamboyant, but after watching his productions you
come away feeling that you really understand each individual
character in a play, and exactly why they act as they do.

'What attracted me towards directing? Well, I suppose it
took me quite a long time to come around to actually
directing plays in the theatre. My interest in that line started
with acting, acting at school and later at university — I was in
a lot of Peter Hall's productions at Cambridge. I didn't really
consider directing at that stage, I did one tiny one-act production of a Tennessee Williams in Cambridge but that was
all. Then when I was in the Army in Hong Kong I did quite a
lot of radio, script-writing, reading the news, disc-jockeying
and so on, and when I came back to England I was torn
between wanting to be an actor and getting into radio in
some sort of way.

'So I joined the BBC and after nine months as a trainee I
got attached to television and was immediately attracted to
the visual side of it, as I had been completely untainted by
television during my childhood. I stayed in television for the
best part of six years, doing mainly documentary work. I
worked on *Monitor* under Huw Wheldon and looked after the
theatre side of it and started off by directing extracts from
plays. While I was working there I started working as well
with a big amateur group called the Tavistock Rep, and again
I acted with them, in John Whiting's *Saint's Day* and in *The
Birthday Party,* and then I started to direct with them and
did about three productions, and out of the blue Peter Hall
asked me to do a production in the Arts Theatre's experimental season in 1962 — *The Empire Builders,* by Boris Vian

— and that was actually my first ever fully professional theatre production.

'Then — it's really quite arbitrary in a way — I knew after I'd done the amateur productions, and that one, that I wanted to do more in the theatre, and in 1964 when BBC2 was just about to open and I'd got to the stage in the BBC when you've become reasonably competent at your job and you find yourself Executive Producer for about three programmes at once, I knew I didn't want that. So when I was offered the chance of joining the RSC, though very much in an administrative capacity, I took it. I was called something very grand, Artistic Controller, and what it amounted to was being Peter Hall's artistic lieutenant and carrying through his executive decisions on the artistic side.

'But I did get a tiny clause in my contract which said I could direct one production a year, however humble, it might be a club night or whatever. After about two years doing purely administrative work I began to fight harder for productions and got more, since when I've moved over more and more to the direction side, though they've hung on to me as an administrator as well, and I've run the Aldwych completely for the last four years until the 1973 season. But I must emphasize that I certainly haven't felt from an early age that I was destined to be a theatre director.

'Now I'm doing it, though I like the combination in directing of a good deal of preparatory research and conceptual ideas about the play, and then the fact that it's really got to be worked out, and even fought out on extreme occasions, in real human terms, vis-à-vis the actors. But I regard the director not as a massive creator of a work of art but above all as a communicator, and your job is to make the text you are handling absolutely crystal-clear, and then it's the function of that particular play to make the experience moving to the audience and the thing really becomes interesting when you have an audience actually sitting in front of a production, when you can gauge whether everything you've set up in rehearsal is actually working or not. Directors — if they're honest — direct a play for themselves to a large extent. During rehearsals you can only be a one-man equivalent of the audience it's going to have. Hopefully, all one's

antennae and human responses to the script and to life if they work for you will work for a lot of other people as well.

'No, I didn't find it difficult to move from television to the theatre, though I know some people find it hard to switch from one medium to the other. I think perhaps because I came to television and films quite late — which though they excite me very much, didn't colour my work or shape it — so coming to the theatre was returning to something I'd already known well when I was younger. It meant I brought some of the standards of television documentary into the theatre. In fact I'm sometimes praised, and often accused that my theatre work is drawn too strongly towards a very detailed naturalism. I wasn't consciously influenced by anyone, though one inherits certain traditions within the RSC of demanding a real non-mystification of a play, the thing has got to stand up in absolutely rational terms of clarity to start with, so that intelligence of production and intelligibility of production are the most important factors. I wouldn't say that any individual director has influenced me — I don't think it's so much that you imitate during your first few productions but that you haven't got the confidence or the experience to push your own ideas through to the absolute hilt. You come more and more round to that stage, and the danger comes when you reach a point when you want every production to be done in the way you would do it, and you can't enjoy other people's work. I think that I admire, in a curious way, those people who don't work like me and I can say, "That's marvellous!" but it wouldn't be the way I would do it. That goes particularly for Peter Hall's early work (I've always thought he was a better director of modern drama than of Shakespeare), and of course Brook, though I would never work in his way. I don't like productions to refer to other productions, and what I try to do when I approach a play is to get rid of the theatrical associations and get back to the life experience and build out of that actuality and reality, then the theatricality in a sense evolves out of that, and not the other way round.

'Admittedly this is difficult with Shakespeare, though I've only done three, *As You Like It, The Tempest* — which is one of those infuriating plays I don't think anyone will ever pull

off, and as soon as the curtain rises on the first night you see
how it should have been done differently — and *Love's
Labour's Lost. Love's Labour's* was good because it's not a
play where the audience knows the big speeches and they
don't have a definitive view of how it should be done. I'm
very keen on narrative, not just the telling of a story but the
fact that it is a bit of human life that evolves from A to Z.
It's so much better for the whole experience if the audience
do not know what is going to happen, so I found something
like Gorky's *Enemies* where the audience don't know the
play and where there is plenty of suspense very good to do,
whereas I watched *Antony and Cleopatra* recently and
although it has some marvellous twists and turns in the
middle section it went for nothing with the audience because
they all know they're both going to die in the end and they
don't respond by getting elated and being put down. I'm sure
an Elizabethan audience that didn't know the story would
have got much more excited than we do now.

'When I set about directing a play I do a great deal of
general preparation now, but not any specific preparation. I
used to do a great deal more brooding as to how exactly I
was going to stage it — and I just don't do any of that any
more. The first and very important creative process is
between you and the designer, and once I've read the play a
couple of times — the first two readings are very seminal —
they set off a lot of explosions, and after that I maybe don't
read the play for three or four weeks, so that everything else
is just coming out of my memory. This is when I start
working with the designer, not giving him a firm brief and
saying "This is what I want," but talking about one's general
response to the play and the general feeling I'd like created,
never "The walls are there and the doors are there," and so
on. I particularly like working with Tim O'Brien, who has a
very strong conceptual sense and it's a very stimulating
process both ways.

'We talk about it three or four times, then Tim will come
up with a definite model, and that both limits and releases
my conception. Even if we throw the original design out, as
soon as I have something concrete there, then I begin to fine
down. That's one side of it, and meanwhile one is doing an

immense amount of research around the world of the play.
For instance, in *Love's Labour's* you're reading about people
of the time, what they read, how they thought, how they
existed. The most difficult thing is to get an actor really to
take the jump of historical imagination which makes the
period of the play so much the present for him that he's
concretely in there, and it's not like a museum-piece where
you observe all the surface details but you don't get the spirit
of the thing.

'For the last three or four productions I've done I haven't
opened the text for the first week of rehearsal, and the
method varies. On the Gorkys we saw an immense number of
Russian films to give them the smell of the period, as it's near
enough for some of it to be on film and also to give them an
idea of what the Russian temperament is like, because when
you first read Gorky what seems like overacting or a very
coarse transition from comedy to self-pity is actually to do
with this very volatile temperament. To get the actors to
switch mood like that was very much easier after seeing the
films. Then with something like Arden's *Island of the Mighty,*
of course there are no films about what it was like in
Arthurian Britain and very little fact, but we spent the first
few days reading what was available in the way of archaeological
and historical researches, then we read a lot of Celtic
mythology, the *Mabinogion* and Celtic poetry.

'Doing it this way, it's partly what you find and partly
what comes out of working with the whole company eight
hours a day. We sit in a vast circle in the rehearsal room and
I don't lecture at all, I pick out pieces from books we've read,
then we read those round the group, which gives them a
chance to actually do something, and after each bit's been
read it's thrown open to the group for comment. It sounds
like a seminar but after five days of that the group, even if
they haven't worked together before, is really concentrating
on the job in hand — they're discovering and sharing the
experience together. In *The Lower Depths,* where I felt we
were a long way from knowing what it was like to be poor or
criminal, we did a lot of delving into our lives and people
were actually coming out with unsavoury stories from their
past, and once they talked quite freely it was interesting to

see how many people had come quite close to something like Gorky in their own lives.

'Then more and more — and I suppose this comes out of confidence — we just start growing from there. When I look back about six years all my copies of plays have little marks and crosses showing each exact move, but now once I've made basic set design decisions, such as in the Gorky, the beds go there and the chairs there, I don't think I had to give a move. Everyone knew exactly where they had to be, it was inevitable. I'd much rather work on an actor's impulse to move or not to move than dictate something. You can get very exciting things out of that, like in Gorky's *Enemies,* when it got to the death of the factory-owner at the end of the first act. We came right up to the run-through and we'd never really blocked that, I'd worked out a batting order in which people should come on, and at the dress rehearsal I arranged when he had to fall across the table, but after that we just improvised from then on and it was marvellous: the danger was that subsequently it should get over-polished. I wanted something jagged, instinctive, almost comic — it couldn't have been consciously choreographed. If an event is *so* strong you can just throw the actors on the stage and it will work the right way.

'I do have a lot of confidence in the actors — I quite like them, actually, contrary to some directors! They're often brave, very vulnerable, and I admire the way they can explore and find things you would never have thought of. I think anyone you work with, cameramen, designers, actors, if they know that you respect their creative contribution and they know you're giving them room to move and you're wanting them to give something, they always work better. You've got to give them a very strong framework to work within, but the sum of twenty-five people being creative in a production is always going to be much better than one. The actor's got to trust you to know that you'll let him take risks in rehearsal but that you'll tell him when it's not working, and when you work with a new actor that's what the first rehearsals are about, establishing a position of trust. Sometimes you can't do it on one production, and sometimes the chemistry never works.

'For instance, the letter scene in *Love's Labour's* was a very good example, the basic geography of that scene I suppose I laid down and who should hide where, then you get actors coming in like the one who plays Dumain. Now he's very keen on singing and he wanted to sing his sonnet because he said, "I'm a very boring reader," and I said, "No, you certainly can't sing it," but when we got as far as running that scene I saw he was very tense about something and he stumbled over the speech so we did it again. I saw the tension building up and he spoke the first four lines and suddenly burst into song exactly as he does it on the stage now. None of us knew he was going to do it and he stared fixedly over my right shoulder convinced I was going to stop him. But the reaction of the other three was absolutely marvellous and I said, "That's great, you can do it." He was so determined I should accept it that he'd done it with a passionate seriousness that worked. Then at a much later stage Bernard Lloyd had the idea of crawling out from behind the tree and making to applaud, then having to check himself and hide again. Now, that's actors creating something. Those are landmarks which come out of an actor being productive at rehearsal and you creating the right atmosphere. Then, finally, when Ian Richardson received the letter the whole thing came together – he is a beautiful manic comedian, and if you set it up for him, he'll take fire out of the situation.

Looking to the future, 'Well, an author I'd very much like to do a play by is Edward Bond. I admire his work very much, though I think it's incredibly difficult to pull off and make it work with an audience because he has got a highly individual, obtuse mind and the jumps he makes and the things he thinks are absolutely clear to everybody, are often very difficult to get over. His style is very cool, very terse and very precise, which I like. He's got not exactly moral ambiguity, because he's absolutely certain where he stands, but a morality which upsets audiences' preconceptions of what is right and what is wrong. He is a deeply moral man who doesn't owe anything to anybody or any system.

'One thing I feel strongly about now is an absolute ruthlessness towards length of material – something that might surprise you after *Island of the Mighty*. I think it's very

easy to be indulgent in the theatre, so I really try to pare
everything down. Within the context of doing way-out stuff
and risky stuff, one must make it all work, and work like a
hammer. Anything that is sloppy, indulgent, goes on too long
and is masturbatory, emotionally, has to go out.'

But he will continue to be drawn to Russian playwrights,
particularly Gorky. 'This comes about through a chain of
events which started with *The Silver Tassie,* then *The
Plebeians Rehearse the Uprising* and finally Gorky, which in
the broadest sense tied in with and echoed the growth of
political awareness in me. Up to *As You Like It,* my approach
was very Freudian. I thought plays were about people passionately and emotionally showing you their insides, then from
*Silver Tassie* and its anti-war theme onwards, a play that just
has an individual ego in the middle but which doesn't explore
the whole society and life around, doesn't interest me very
much. Now I want to do plays that encompass a whole social
attitude and have an awareness of social and political tensions
between the people in them.'

# James Cellan Jones

James Cellan Jones is the only director in this book who is
not primarily a theatre director. In fact, he is best known for
his work on television. The reason I have included him is
because he of all people currently working in that medium
has provided me with the kind of excitement that I usually
associate only with the live theatre. Watching television is a
peripheral activity, something I tend to do on nights when I
do not have to go to the theatre, and it is rare indeed for me
to stay in and watch a whole series of plays, let alone to do
that for thirteen weeks as I did with his production *Roads to
Freedom.*

He is a large, softly spoken Welshman with a gentle wit.
Like some of the others, he rather drifted into direction.
'When I was at school I used to act a little bit — I didn't go
to a very artistic school — but when I went into the Army to
do my National Service I got the job of organizing a concert
party, which was rather funny to us, as we were all suffering
a lot and hating it all. I wrote a lot of the numbers for it, and
the only way I was able to get peace and quiet to write at all
was in the lavatory, the only place they didn't chase you. We
put it on in a tented camp, lit it with tilley lamps stuck in
biscuit tins, and built a stage. I suppose that was the first time
you could say I'd truly directed, and that was purely because
the others left it to me because they hadn't got a clue.

'I knew I'd always wanted to do something in the theatre. I
suppose I was later than most people, certainly later than
people are nowadays deciding what they want to do. They
seem to know exactly what they're doing and where they're
going from the age of about fifteen. I suppose those of us
who had to do National Service did have a problem, for it
meant that people had to delay for a long time deciding
what career to take up because they knew it would be interrupted and they didn't want to settle on something which

was going to be blown apart." When I came out of the Army I
went into the BBC as a call boy. I had, I suppose, would-be
noble intentions of working my way up. It took what
seemed an awful long time — seven years. First I was assistant
floor manager, then floor manager, then production assistant,
and finally I was allowed to do some directing, mostly a lot
of rubbish. Gradually they allowed me to do what I wanted,
but as soon as ever I could, I got out from under the BBC
contract.'

In fact, in his first attempt at directing he was marking out
a pattern he would be following for years, that of a director
of classic serials. 'One day I was suddenly told to go off to
Exmoor and shoot twenty minutes of snow scenes for *Lorna
Doone.* I read the book, designed the costumes, wrote a
shooting script and took a unit into blizzards all in two days
. . . . I and the unit played the parts, doubling for actors not
yet cast, and my most vivid memory is staggering across virgin
snow with a sheep under each arm — no remakes because of
the footmarks.'

Sometimes writers come to him with an idea, 'but in a
strange way, some of the most successful work I've done has
been when I've been second choice for directing a play. In
fact, with some of those early serials, like Stendhal's *Scarlet
and Black,* I was third or fourth choice — of course, I didn't
know that, I thought I was first.'

A director working on film has problems very different
from those of a theatre director. Taking *Roads to Freedom*
as an example of how he works, the job began months
before filming started. 'David Turner, the writer, and I worked
hard for about eighteen months to two years before anything
was actually put on paper, because there were so many
decisions that had to be made, especially what was left in and
what was taken out. For instance, in the middle novel, *The
Reprieve,* there are twenty different threads, they're all
marvellous and some of them have got to go. In the book the
narrative continues, then stops, then another takes over from
it, and you're continually going back and finding out where
you left off, and you can't do that in visual narrative. So I
had to fine it down to the main characters and those who
crossed their paths; I nearly broke my heart leaving out some

of the people and some of the situations — but they had to go.

'Then comes the basic research, such as finding the districts and the streets, for Sartre is very specific, then David Turner wrote the episodes very, very quickly. I forget just how quickly he managed those thirteen episodes — and I looked at them, but I didn't need to do very much to them, because by that time we both knew where we were going; then came the frenzied period of casting 116 speaking parts.'

'A basic difference between film and theatre is that film is usually shot out of sequence, and you can actually begin filming at the end of the story. Funnily enough, that's not as difficult as it sounds, especially on television; so long as you've been able to rehearse the whole thing it doesn't matter if you start at the beginning, the end or in the middle, you have the feeling of the structure, you feel you know it and haven't just been dumped in the middle somewhere. I find rehearsals in filming are vitally important, and still aren't done very much. (People wander in without rehearsal and just start from cold, but I won't have that.) Even if you only have a week's rehearsal you're miles ahead, and on a major production I try to have three, then film on location, then rehearse, then do a block of studio, rehearse, go back on location and so on.

'But the exciting thing about television is that if you can get a cast together and develop this mutual trust thing, it's absolute dynamite. They get to know each other so well that they find themselves completing each other's sentences and knowing exactly what each other's doing before you tell them. In a way, it's more of an ensemble company than those who set out to build one with that aim in mind, when it can be incredibly incestuous. I think, let's be corny and call it that kind of brotherhood thing, has got to arrive by chance, it's very difficult to plan for. If you say, "Now we're going to turn ourselves self-consciously into an ensemble during the next fifteen weeks' rehearsal" you're going to find at the end of that time that you've a company of mentally aggressive people with one or two on the brink of suicide and one or two more who are just about ready to shoot some of the others. In fact we did with the actors on the Sartre serial for a long time — nine months — and you can get the kind of

incident where we found ourselves pushed for time and
wanting to shoot a very difficult scene on the banks of the
Seine. We could have done it in the studio with eight
reflected-off water trays, but instead we finished filming on
the Saturday afternoon, flew to Paris, worked from five in
the morning till nine at night, flew back and started
immediately on the next day's work. If I hadn't had actors
who were in advance of what they were doing, then it
wouldn't have been possible.'

Working methods? 'I don't think a big lecture on the day
of the first rehearsal is any good. I think you must let them
make mistakes, try all kinds of things and then discuss the
characters as they go along. I'm a great believer in actors who
work by instinct. Eileen Atkins, for instance, who was in my
production of *The Dream,* will say that some move doesn't
feel right. I'll let her try what her instinct suggests, but then
we'll take it apart afterwards while we discover why the new
move is right.

'One is always asked what other directors have influenced
you. It makes me feel like a multi-plagiarist! It's very difficult,
very hard to say, but I know I was very influenced by the
work of Michael Elliott when I started in television. He now
does very little television and no films, but he was one of the
most extraordinary talents working in the medium. I was
young and aggressive and working my way up, and long
before he did any theatre he came straight into television
from Oxford as a director, which is a thing one naturally
resents, but one couldn't resent it because however important
professionalism is — and I'm hooked on professionalism —
there is no substitute for talent, and someone who is very
talented can just come striding in and immediately do good
work. As for other influences, I did an interview once where
they used stills from work I'd done with hideously intellectually
embarrassing captions, such as "Godard-like lighting in this
shot," "See the Truffaut influence in the geometric thing" —
you know, it may or may not be true but it was very
embarrassing.'

He likes using actors he knows well. 'If you do that then
you can start by standing on the shoulders of past productions,
which is a tremendous advantage and your actors have already

related to you as an individual and don't have to start from scratch. They're people I've enjoyed working with over the years, though they tend to be called "the James Cellan Jones Repertory Company". I use a lot of National Theatre and RSC actors because some of them tend to be very under-used.

When he does direct for the stage — for example, Birmingham Rep's production of *St Joan* — then he does find difficulties. 'For example, I've always been interested in lighting but one hasn't had ever to physically decide what lamps should be used and work out cues, one's just put one's oar in, but in the theatre you're told, "You're directing it, you light it, and mark the cues and all the rest of it," which was very good for me. In a sense it was a great sort of liberation because I was able to do non-realistic things on the stage which I couldn't have done on film or television; in *Joan*, for instance, for the Banks of the Loire scene I covered the stage with dry ice and lit it peculiarly so that when it started the two little figures were there absolutely isolated in the mist and it made the stage seem much bigger.'

Although he is a man who describes himself as 'pathologically non-violent' he is fascinated by the problems of violence. 'Once I was physically attacked by a member of the audience when doing a TV programme. I just had to stand there and let it happen; I kept getting hit and the man spat at me, full in the face. It seemed to last forever and I needed a stiff drink afterwards.' But it's something he keeps coming back to, especially the immediate pre-War era in which both *Roads to Freedom* and *Eyeless in Gaza* are set. 'It's a period I find fascinating; people affected by the rise of Fascism.' The other thread that runs through his work, and is there in a film he wants to do, is that of the introverted man searching for a reason for living and for an identity, usually coupled with an inability to communicate or form any kind of strong personal relationship. 'The film I hope to do one day is called *The Night I Caught the Santa Fé Chief,* by Edward Thorpe — an extraordinary first novel about a rather effete Englishman who has a car crash in the desert and eventually gets picked up by a bank robber who at first thinks he's a criminal and then takes him as a hostage. They go off across the desert and live rough and there's a weird surprise ending. What attracts me to it is again the search for freedom, and while there's some marvellous scenic stuff and all that, the search is the germ of the thing, that and the relationship growing between them in the few words they say to each other. They're both inarticulate. It would have to be a low-budget picture, and that would be right as it would be ruined if a lot of money was spent on it.'

He finds a low budget and a sense of pressure can be a creative influence. 'I do work best under pressure, but it can go too far. I think a certain financial pressure is always useful — I mean that in both senses, that you need the money and that you've got a limited budget — but if it goes too far then things get very tatty, and demonstrate that not enough money has been spent. If you've too little time it just looks shoddy, but just too little time, perhaps a day less than you really need, then that's just about right.'

But, finally, there is one place you will never find him — Hollywood. 'I went there twice to promote a film. It's a weird place, absolutely weird, it's not of this world. I would loathe to live and work there. I mean, it's very easy to be superficial about it and say of course people are obsessed with money and status; it's not only that, it's the fact that it is a town built not on films but on success in films, and they don't reckon actors, they only reckon stars, and success is horribly important. I just found it an appalling place, even though there are a lot of good people there, but it's such a lousy atmosphere to work in, so utterly removed from life. Unless your work has some contact with ordinary life, then it isn't going to bear any relation to it.'

# Joan Littlewood

If you try to ask Joan Littlewood about the art of theatre at
the moment you are likely to get thrown out on your neck.
Unlike the others, she is battling for sheer survival. Mindless
planning has led to a repellent development scheme which
must have been designed to squeeze the Theatre Royal out
and have it pulled down.

The multi-storey office blocks now tower over the theatre
building, its forecourt is used as a dumping-place for rubbish
and as an unofficial car-park for lorries and bulldozers and
the noise of pneumatic drills and concrete mixers goes on all
day. Even with all the doors and windows shut the actors can
hardly hear themselves rehearse, and the filth and dirt from
the building-site pours into the theatre through cracks and
crannies. Joan has spent literally days shovelling filth out of
the cellar under the stage to try to make space for costumes,
and is fast giving up hope.

Theatre buffs and even the Establishment pay lip-service
to what she has done for British theatre, especially with
*Oh, What a Lovely War,* but when you see the conditions in
which she has to work you realize that they just do not care.

'It's disgusting, it makes me feel sick. Do you remember
what it was like here with the little houses and the market
in Angel Lane? The market itself was theatre with the lights,
the stalls, the colours and, most of all, the people. There were
the costers with names like Ivry which went back for genera-
tions. This kind of thing here takes no account of people's
lives.

'I'd rather go back on the road. I like the Bedouin concept
of doing a show and then moving on somewhere else. When
we used to visit the mining villages years ago we'd move in
and decorate the streets and do up the village hall and the
people would come in and enjoy it. I'm not really a theatre
indoors person. We got this Bedouin technique to its peak

in Paris and I felt this is what I'd wanted to do all my life. Then I felt I ought to do something here and came back.'

After the days of *Lovely War* and *Sparrers Can't Sing,* in 1962, she tried to get her schemes off the ground for a fun palace, and for pleasure gardens in the Lea Valley, but they came to nothing. 'You talk to me about theatre, the Lea Valley would have been theatre, it would have been what Vauxhall Gardens used to be in the eighteenth and nineteenth centuries, with music and theatre and fireworks and all kinds of things going on. It was a ground-plan for change, but it was too big a concept for anyone to have the imagination to do it.'

When the plans came to nothing she went off to Tunisia and settled down on twenty acres, 'where I had the time of my life working in a kind of theatre that had nothing at all to do with the pros. arch and nineteenth century buildings'.

But the East End drew her back. If the Theatre Royal is bulldozed flat and Joan leaves there will be no professional theatre east of central London until you reach Hornchurch. 'They think people here are cabbageheads. They drive out through Stratford to their houses in the country, to the coast at weekends, and they shut their eyes and they don't even see what it is like any more. It is remarkable how people can close their eyes to things when they want to. These awful buildings aren't even going to be homes, they're offices and car parks. We're being buried alive.'

All her outbuildings and storage spaces have been bulldozed flat. Her efforts to entertain local children during the school holidays by using an old school building for painting, music, drama and a library were stopped and she was told the building was needed for 'development'. It is still unused. The space outside the theatre where she wanted gardens and a children's playground is just a rubbish heap surrounded by barbed wire. 'I needed the space for the kids because this is all part of the theatre; what happens on the stage inside the building is only one part of it. I felt ashamed, though, at Christmas. We had twenty-five thousand children in here to see *Christmas Carol,* and with the work going on outside the building shook so much I literally thought it would collapse.'

1972-3 saw a number of new, light-hearted Littlewood shows, *Costa Packet,* about a package holiday to Spain,

*So You Want To Be In Pictures,* and *Gentlemen Prefer
Anything* which carries the standard for women's lib. They
have had a mixed reception, but on the whole have been
well received critically, and they have gone down very well
with the local audiences. 'Though what went down best was
when we opened the theatre for three nights and had local
variety acts for three or four hours and maths games and
people reciting poetry and so on. I don't really know
whether I liked it or not but it was very interesting, and
people kept coming up to me afterwards in the street and
saying they hadn't had a night out like that for ages.

'Perhaps the only function of theatre is as a cheer-up in
this life.' It was only in 1972 that she managed to get an
Arts Council grant. 'Locally they don't think we were
worth it because of what we did — it's a kind of ghastly
inverted snobbery — and the Arts Council didn't think we
rated as culture. Culture is going to the Queen Elizabeth
Hall on a Saturday night or to the theatre to see Marianne
Faithful in *Uncle Vanya.* That's culture, that is.'

The other basic problem is getting actors and stage staff to
work in conditions which are something akin to troop theatre
on the Somme battlefield. 'You can't ask people to come here
and try and work in all this noise. And I scrub out the stage
and cellars because I don't feel I can ask anyone to do such a
dreadful job. People get all sentimental about Theatre
Workshop and talk about *Oh, What a Lovely War* and say the
building mustn't be pulled down and all that but what am I
supposed to do, how am I supposed to work?

'People who talk about all my good work in the past don't
want to come here now. It could be made a bit better if we
had more room and if at least we could do something at the
front, have gardens and trees and a kids' playground. All
those little back-to-back houses which used to be here had
marvellous little gardens. The man of the house could be
Capability Brown in miniature if he wanted to be. Now it's
just a waste land and the only positive action which has
been taken is the police coming to fingerprint the kids to
find out who has been playing on it. When I look around I'm
not surprised about the teenage vandalism and violence, I'm
surprised people remain so gentle.'

Joan, as she says herself, is unlikely to be popular with the
artistic establishment, 'because I tend to be rude to them
when I meet them.' She is, indeed, very rude on occasion,
with a shattering frankness which raises the hair on the heads
of her friends as well as her enemies. Also her working
methods are very peculiar to her, and I once came across a
young actress sitting crying in the foyer, 'because Joan's gone
and changed the words and the moves again'. Actors who are
used to working with Joan accept her constant rearrangements
placidly, as they do the roaring rages and sprinklings of four-
letter words. But she says, proudly and truthfully, 'I pay my
actors more than many repertory companies which are far,
far better off. At least I pay thirty to forty pounds a week,
some of the others pay the basic Equity minimum, as little
as they can.'

Joan, as she admits, will never be able to go to the Arts
Council with a nicely organized season in which every production has been costed out to the last penny, but for God's sake,
should this matter? Her large and original talent towers over
the subsidized theatre, and that she should be reduced to
spending all her energy trying to keep going instead of on
creative work is a national disgrace. When I interviewed Anton
Wajda he said he had two things to do when he came to
England, to go to Stratford in Warwickshire and see the Royal
Shakespeare Company, and to go to Stratford East and meet
Joan.

If she was given all she asked she would remain pig-headed,
stubborn and difficult, but then this is true of all originals.
She won't ever greet her first-night audiences in an evening
dress or scour the newspaper columns on New Year's Day to
see if she is in the Honours List. But if she spent all her Arts
Council grant on Guinness and drank herself into oblivion
she remains, with Peter Cheeseman, the only director who has
tried to bring about an entirely new relevant form of subsidized theatre. And it has beaten her down. 'All we want',
she says, 'is a place to breathe. I get so tired because I have
to keep fighting for the same things, not even to go forward,
but to stop being driven back.'

# Jonathan Miller

Jonathan Miller has virtually the most untheatrical background of all his colleagues. His subject was medicine, and he arrived in the theatre almost by chance.

'I got into directing by accident. I wasn't intending to work at it at all. I had just finished *Beyond the Fringe* in London, and George Devine was looking for someone to direct one half of a double bill of John Osborne plays, a play called *Under Plain Cover,* which I believe had been hawked around all over London and none of the established directors wanted to do it, so they scraped the bottom of the barrel looking for someone who might have some kind of odd idea and thought that one of us from *Beyond the Fringe* might be the one to direct it. As I had six or seven weeks to spare before we took the show to America, and had nothing to lose anyway, I took it on. I did it without knowing anything about directing, or being particularly interested in it, or the theatre in general.

'I did the play and it was quite successful and I enjoyed the experience very much, then I forgot about it. I went to America and did *Beyond the Fringe* and didn't think anything more about it. About eighteen months later, Robert Lowell, a friend of mine in New York, produced a play based on some stories of Melville and Hawthorne, and he again had hawked it around to a number of established directors, including those at the Actors Studio, who didn't want to do it; they didn't like it very much. I rather liked it, and a group called the Players Theatre asked me to do it. That was a great success, and then I thought I might like to do the work and do it properly.

'Although again when I came back to England I didn't do any theatre for years. I went into television, doing things like *Monitor,* films like *Alice in Wonderland* and some on Plato's dialogues. I decided it would be quite nice to do some theatre properly, so I went to the RSC and asked Peter Hall if he

would give me a chance to direct a play there, and he was
going to let me do *Measure for Measure,* and then the management changed and he left but he suggested I should train
myself more fully in the classical theatre and told me to go
to a provincial rep, and as Stuart Burge was looking for
somebody for the Nottingham Playhouse, I went there. I did
*The School for Scandal* there, then *The Seagull,* then *King
Lear.* So I found myself working almost full time in the
theatre. I did another Robert Lowell play, *Prometheus
Bound,* at Yale with Irene Worth and Kenneth Haigh, then
some amateur Shakespeare with the Oxford and Cambridge
group, doing *Twelfth Night, Julius Caesar* and *Hamlet,* by
which time I felt familiar with Shakespeare and was invited
to the National by Oliver, where I did *The Merchant of
Venice, Danton's Death* and *School for Scandal.* Suddenly I
was up to my neck in full-time theatre work.

'At this time, however, I was working as a research Fellow
in the history of medicine at University College, so I had to
divide my time between that any my work as a director.
Now my Fellowship is coming to an end and I'm an associate
director of the National; I've just done an opera by
Alexander Goehr called *Arden Must Die*. I did finally get
around to doing *Measure for Measure* as a mobile for the
National — it's been a heavy year.

'What do I enjoy working on most? Really the thing I'm
doing at the moment — I very rarely think about the future,
though I've vague ideas about plays I'd like to do. I'd like to
work all the way through the Shakespeare canon. I don't
want to work on modern plays at the moment, for several
reasons, because to get a good modern play that's worth
doing you have to read about eight or nine hundred plays
before you find one that is even worth looking at. The
advantage of doing classical plays is that history's done the
laborious task of reading for you, so you have a sieve which
has taken out the nonsense and left you with the good plays.
As I don't enjoy reading plays I find it easier to pick out
the classical canon, and I also find there are very few plays
worth doing, apart from Shakespeare, Chekhov, Ibsen and
perhaps Pirandello or Brecht, and one's time can be fully
occupied working backwards and forwards on that system.

If a marvellous modern play came along and fell into my
lap I would do it.

'There are other reasons why I do plays from the past. One
of them is the fact that the author is dead. People often
accuse me of this and say he only likes to work with an
author who's dead because he's a coward, and an iconoclast,
and likes to break plays up, and only with a dead author are
you able to do this, and actually I'm not frightened of that
accusation. I prefer to work with dead authors precisely
because they can't give you an argument. I don't believe one
has any duty or obligation to an author, once he's dead. I
think the concept of the public domain is very important in
art, and that when a work in the performing arts has been
finished, after the first, second or third try, during which I
think one owes it to the author to honour his explicit
conscious intention, and to co-operate with him and try and
imagine it as it was when he wrote it, then after that it enters
this curious zone of the public area and his aesthetic rights in
it lapse. The play becomes a public object and one should be
able to do to it exactly what one wants to.

'The only rules to apply are those of aesthetic consistency,
formal elegance and accuracy and artistic finesse, and that
need have no bearing on what the author actually meant. We
have no idea really what Shakespeare *meant* in his plays, he
didn't write prefaces, thank God; he didn't leave very formal
stage instructions, he just gives you a series of speeches which
are made by certain characters. Of course they're not real
characters, you haven't been introduced to them, there are
no biographical details about them. You can infer a biography
of some sort from what they say and do to each other but
the interesting thing about great characters in drama is that
you can infer a whole series of quite contradictory biographies,
all of which are consistent with the text, and all of which are
incompatible with one another. There are eight hundred
different Hamlets.

'Bernard Williams the philosopher said that what makes the
difference between a real person and a character in fiction or
drama is that it makes no sense to ask for further details about
a character in drama, not because they're hard to rootle out
or obtain but because they're non-existent and the whole

point of producing a play is improvizing a biography which is consistent with the utterances that they make in the play, and the remarkable thing is that you can infer an infinite series of biographies, and that really is the fun of directing, trying to find out these biographical alternatives. But you can't do that unless you feel absolutely free and unobliged to the author. Obviously there are certain things which are incompatible with the text — there are no rules for it. As you go along you just alter and mould and shape the production so that it remains consistent with what the character seems to be saying, but it's very hard to find out what he is saying.

'This is what rehearsal is. It's very much like a spiritualistic seance where you heat the atmosphere up to the point where a voice starts to speak through the text which the author has provided and as you listen you begin to hear the accents and tones of a person to whom you've never been introduced, but who is nevertheless using those particular utterances to make himself understood. If the rehearsal goes well and it is congenial then these voices are conjured up very readily. You're surprised to find that new and unexpected characters are speaking through these lines, but you have to use the lines as things through which characters speak rather than prepared speeches, the characters for which are already established. They become established in the process of finding out who they are. It is like a seance — they are absconded personalities each of these characters. You have no idea who Hamlet is, but gradually in the course of rehearsal, someone who might be Hamlet speaks these lines so consistently that you accept that personality as a convincing claimant to the title of Hamlet.'

One aspect of his work which has either pleased or annoyed his critics is that of setting Shakespeare plays in particular in another age, *The Merchant* in the late nineteenth century, *Measure for Measure* in the twenties. 'I like playing tricks with time, occasionally it's an interesting thing to do. One sometimes gets attacked for doing this, it's thought to be a gimmick but the people who attack you very rarely look at Shakespeare, who was doing it all the time. He was always playing tricks with time, Roman characters speak Tudor English, *King Lear* is set in a pre-Christian England with characters who couldn't be anything other than Christians. So that as a director one takes one's cue from Shakespeare, or indeed from any of the European artists of the last five hundred years who move back and forth in time and set their plays in different periods, and in much the same way one sets Shakespeare in different periods so as to emphasize certain features of the plot which wouldn't be apparent in the period in which Shakespeare nominally sets the play.

'So when I decided to do a Victorian production of *The Merchant* I was thinking of certain other literary overtones which would react with the play, certain relationships which would come out more strongly if brought into the Victorian period such as the relationship between Antonio and Bassanio which was very much like that between Oscar Wilde and Lord Alfred Douglas. Portia was rather a Jamesian heroine, and by putting the production into that period the particular sides of the characters began to expand and complicate in such a way that the play became interesting in another way. It would be foolish to pretend it was a definitive version   I don't think there is such a thing, it's simply another shot at a play.

'I often start a play with a kind of still photograph in my mind, often without any clear-cut social ideas. Those begin to condense and grow around the photograph. I started *The Merchant* having seen a collection of photographs of Venice, Milan and Rome in the 1890s, and they were etched on my imagination and recurred in my mind's eye. Gradually the literary associations of the period began to condense around those photographs and I became convinced it would be a good period to set it in.

'When it came to *Measure for Measure,* I was prompted there not so much by a positive image of the 1920s in Vienna so much as a determination not to set it in that somewhat pre-Raphaelite Tudor period. The Victorians for some reason took a great interest in the play, the chaste piety of Isabella excited their imagination. I was repelled by that sort of story-telling piety where she becomes a chaste, beautiful heroine, repellent and rather impenetrable. So I looked for an alternative period in which her character could become understandable, and the word Vienna struck my imagination, and I was thinking of the whole idea of the decaying Habsburg city. So I set it in the Vienna which happened to coincide with that of Freud, not because I wanted to make any specific references but because it was a good period in which there was doubt about authority and the individual, the conflict between religion and personal morality, and again I'd been looking at photographs taken by Auguste Sander and it just seemed a good container to put the thing inside. It began to work, she became rather an interesting girl, she became neurotic rather than a moral emblem.

'I am interested in the visual aspect of the play. I've worked with Pat and Rosemary Robertson ever since I was at Nottingham, and with others, such as Julia Oman, but especially the Robertsons. We understand each other, and use the same language. I do have a strong influence on the design because I'm very interested in the history of painting and in photography and in stage design, so I start with a very clear visual image of what I would like it to be, then I discuss this with the designer and eventually it takes shape. I get more ideas from painting and the history of art criticism than I do from the theatre. I don't go very much to the theatre — I can't get any ideas from productions that are worth looking at because if they are then they've already completed an idea. I get most of my ideas from reading outside the area of drama which seems a reasonable and important thing to do; if you draw your ideas only from within drama you get inbreeding and eventually haemophilia.

'I suppose the sources I draw upon more than anything, apart from intuition, are the history of art, history and social anthropology. I'm more influenced by social anthropology than anything — so many of Shakespeare's plays are dealing with issues which the anthropologists have opened out that I would find it difficult to do these plays without the insight anthropology has given me.'

Directors seem to divide themselves into those who feel happier working within a company and those who prefer freelancing. 'I enjoy the repertory set-up. I don't think it's essential, I think there's a lot of dogma about companies, but equally there's a lot of foolish dogma about stars. I think it's possible to create an ensemble spirit in one production with actors who've never met, so long as you choose actors who are open, convivial, friendly, co-operative and uncompetitive. You will effectively create an ensemble if the work is interesting. Almost all directors tend to have a phantom repertory company, say twenty or thirty actors, in their mind's eye, who they will tend to call on again and again, and there are actors I've worked with a lot, but I don't think the strict repertory situation is essential. I don't think there's any rule about this. I like having a home, a base; what I don't like about working as a director is the tinker aspect of it. It's a restless life, and very bad simply for domestic living. I'd be happy to work in the same place for the rest of my life.

'I can't work in the commercial theatre, I don't like the pressures of West End managements nor the kind of plays they would insist on putting on. I don't like the star system — stars are the death of good theatre. They may be very remarkable, but they glitter and glare and they're so competitive and peculiar that you find you are catering for their requirements and they leave a fallout around them in a production.

'I like good actors — I don't like great ones. I think there's something very damaging about great actors. They have usually become great through the exploitation of some peculiar or vulgar effect. I prefer a modest intelligence and diligence, a modest inventiveness, to greatness. What you want in a play is a feeling of a whole life lived, and when that's done properly you can't really say at the end of the time that you've seen a good performance, you've simply been aware of the fact that something splendid has happened. I just don't like great actors — you're always deferring to them, and when you're deferring to them you're usually neglecting the others, and that may produce a dazzling evening in the theatre for an audience but in the end they've been cheated, they've had a circus performance, a high-wire act, and the other actors have been used for holding safety nets or else dressed in satin, standing in the ring holding their hands up pointing to the star. England is *filled* with good actors, amazing performers, attentive, inventive, vivid and careful.

'There are all kinds of things I'd like to do in the theatre which I can't because they're too expensive; not expensive in terms of sets, I hate elaborate visual forms in the theatre, but what I would really like to do is to perform all the Shakespeare tragedies in an extremely small theatre, or in a room, I like the idea of hearing Shakespeare spoken quietly. So much gets denatured by being projected, not necessarily shouted but simply projected into a theatre where there are more than a hundred people. I would like to do *King Lear* in a room not much larger than this, with an audience of about sixty who are never more than twenty or thirty feet from an actor. There's a moment in a production before the dress rehearsal when you just do a run-through, when the play is always at its very best, and it's always downhill from then on. That is the moment when it reaches that absolutely naked, raw form which is what the theatre ought to be like, and it's when we're using ordinary tables and chairs and people are sitting talking to each other. Ultimately that is what the theatre is about — about belief being totally suspended and at its strongest form, and this is when people are without costumes and props, for this is where your imagination is being taxed. The moment when someone comes in in an ordinary pair of trousers and sits and talks to somebody else and is claiming to be King Lear and convinces you he is, this is when his art is working at its most intense. If he's convincing you he's Lear only because he's wearing the costume of a king the level on which he is operating as an actor is obviously much, much lower. So I'd like to do things simply in small spaces, but that's the most expensive theatre there is. The expense isn't the costumes and sets but the proportion of audience to cast.

'Ultimately what I think there ought to be is — and we're ripe for it — a Protestant Reformation in theatre, a non-conformist enthusiasm in the theatre, small, intense local congregations all over England where actors perform for no more than a hundred people at a time. I think they all ought to be called the National Theatre, in exactly the same way the National Health Service isn't localized at St Thomas's Hospital, but it's everywhere. There should be some kind of qualification which allows an actor to be a member of the National Theatre which would have, say, three or four hundred actors who would be performing anywhere from

Pitlochry to Southampton. But the idea of having it
congregated in some gigantic cathedral, a sort of Basil
Spence new Coventry on the South Bank, seems to me to
be a bad idea theatrically and a ridiculous idea socially.
That is why I'm so glad that the third auditorium at the
New National will be for plays which need to be done in a
small theatre, not because they go there to be tried out to
see if they can be done somewhere else but because that's
the place that is best for them. It's rather like saying that
Beethoven's Quartets, having qualified, should be performed
at Wembley.

'Experimental theatre so called holds no charms for me, I
don't know what it means. I don't think you can experiment
in the theatre, there's not that much room to experiment.
I'm a scientist, and I was taught what experiments really
are, and there's no room for that in the theatre.

'There's a great dogma around at the moment about non-
verbal forms in the theatre and somehow that the use of
language is degenerate, or a corrupt piece of capitalist
property; that language is the property of the Establishment
and the simple, the primitive and the *folk* is really what
theatre is about, and that underneath the spoken language
there is another form of communication, much richer, hotter
and more communicative than anything we do in terms of
words. That seems to me to be absolute balls. Language is
the leading edge of the human personality, it's the only form
of communication in which we can express the subtle dis-
criminations which make us different from animals, and
different from savages. I don't think that civilization is a
degeneration from savagery, and I think anything which
refines and makes language more accurate is a better form
of theatre. This doesn't mean I want to see all theatre
reduced to radio, it has to be given the forms we normally
do by using our hands, clothes and lights but if you remove
language and only have clothes, gestures and lights it's
simply like having a body without a skeleton. Language is
the flexible skeleton of the human imagination.

'The non-verbal theatre comes from a basic anti-intellectual
conception of the human imagination. Language is our most
basic and characteristic competence. The idea that there is a

sort of language that all people speak, and that the Tower of
Babel was a catastrophe, is biological and anthropological
nonsense. There is no way of speaking to someone without
using the code that he, as a member of that language community, has learned — the idea that you can bypass that
code and go downstairs to a code to which all human beings
have access is a piece of eighteenth-century romanticism
which is just rubbish.

'Therefore the idea of going off to speak to Africans or
Indians in some form of supposedly primeval language means
absolutely nothing. It's illogical, it's absurd and I think it
springs ultimately from illiteracy, from not reading enough,
not finding out about what the human brain is like. Theatre
is a very serious experimental work in the scientific sense —
not in the sense of trying innovations, but it's a very interesting technique to find out what the human brain does. This
is why I moved so easily from medicine into theatre, it's
medicine carried on by other means. If you don't treat it
as part of culture in general, then it's a frivolous exercise.

'Otherwise you might as well put on ice shows or Talk of
the Town, it's absolutely meaningless, it's camp. I sometimes
think that this kind of theatre is dressed up show-biz camp.
Everything that human beings have done that distinguish us
from the animals comes from our capacity to use language.
It's the duty of everyone who works in the theatre to honour
language first and foremost. Ballet and mime are a jejune
form of art, you only suffer them on the understanding that
they are abstentions from the main task, which is language. If
you say you reach a larger audience without using language
you might say you reach even more people by tickling them
with ostrich feathers. You reach a large number of people at
a crude biological level.

'Otherwise one gets to the absurd proposition that somehow Chekhov is degenerate but an Indian rain dance is the
best. Indian rain dances, rather than being an expression of
a noble form of life, are a rather pathetic demonstration of
an incompetent group of people handling an overwhelming
environment over which they have no control in a crude
and infantile way. I think we're more interesting than they
are. I can't bear this frightful cultural primitivism that's

broken out now.

'It all goes along with astrology and palmistry and the occult and all these terrible practices which are a terrible *trahison de chair.* I really do feel that intellectuals in the theatre who have abdicated their responsibility to civilization and the higher forms of human communications are, in fact, traitors who have committed treason of a very, very dreadful sort. We owe it to ourselves to honour the highest forms of our expression.

'You get this frightful bearded student thing of, "Wow, man, it's all part of the whole — you know, capitalist stuff, you know! a mere lovin' bit . . . ." It seems to me there are landmarks where the human imagination has demonstrated itself very distinctively, and I think that in the manufacture of something like a Vermeer or the *Origin of Species,* the formulation of the theory of gravitation, or the writing of *Hamlet* and *Othello* it is something more distinctive and more interesting than anything which is done by a group of men in war-paint stamping round a fire and hoping it will rain next day. If Newton had tried to explain the theory of gravitation by putting on paint and gesturing wildly at the Fellows of the Royal Academy we would never have got anywhere.

'The thing about language is that it actually says something, it makes assertions about the world; you cannot, wagging a bamboo pole and with bizarre makeup and with a lot of groans and hums, tell anything about a scene which is not immediately there. You cannot recall the past, recall a memory, you cannot indicate anxieties about the future, the whole thing about language is that you can express subtle discriminating varieties of anxiety about the future. You couldn't express anxiety about twenty years hence with a bamboo pole. Language is the only way we can make propositions about things, and that's what makes us interesting and different, otherwise you get this idea that animals are human beings with very bad speech defects and if one could only get down to the cat's language one would be communicating with the Universe — the reason cats can't talk isn't because we don't know their language, it's because they haven't got anything to say.'

# *Trevor Nunn*

From grammar school to the director of the Royal Shakespeare Company, in a single bound, might seem something
of an exaggeration, but certainly Trevor Nunn's career
has been singularly successful. He went from Cambridge to
the Belgrade in his late twenties, when the mantle of Peter
Hall became his — a forbidding task. Hailed as the protagonist
of the ensemble theatre, his own ideas have modified during
his time with the RSC.

He became stage-struck while still at school in Ipswich, his
home town, where he saw his first plays at the Arts Theatre.

'The Ipswich Theatre is a perfect example of how the
provincial repertory movement has changed. When I was a
kid I went to the Ipswich Arts Theatre regularly. Is it just
the trick of memory or was it adolescent enthusiasm that
makes that work seem now so lucid, so original and so
accomplished? There was a semi-permanent company, it had
Val May as artistic director (followed by Peter Coe, then
Anthony Richardson), and the standard of the work was —
as I remember it — very high. It was there I saw my first
Shakespeare play, *The Taming of the Shrew*. Paul Eddington
played Petruchio. I went with a bunch of school-kids, we
were about twelve years old, and for the first time I encoun-
tered something exclusive about that theatre. The actors
relished the school-kids in the stalls, brought them into the
performance. I performed bits of the play weeks afterwards.
I wanted to play Grumio.

'It was there I saw *Othello* for the first time. David Waller
played Iago. I can understand how theatre traditions come
about. If I were a Hazlitt I could write ten pages, not only
about the general shape of his performance but about details
of it, nuances of it, how he said certain words. It was a very
startling creation, a dark *en brosse* head, a savage, scowling,
military bullneck, a vicious sense of humour. It's the only

time I have been aware of the military detail that abounds in the play, until John Barton's version two years ago. I queued up at the stage door for David Waller's autograph. Then I had a unique experience, dreamlike really. I actually got to work at the theatre.

'They were doing a production of *Life with Father,* that American evergreen. The youngest member of the family is Harlan, who is about ten years old, and at the age of thirteen I went through a series of auditions and was eventually cast. Local boy makes good. That was the most life-changing, or life-focusing, moment of my youth.

'Although I'd frequently declared to my family that I was going to be a great actor, I was going to be involved in the theatre, be a comedian and so on, that was really the first time when I understood it was possible to be part of that world instead of being a spectator and having fantasies about it. The play was tremendously successful, and I was given a great deal of coverage in the local Press as a kind of infant prodigy. That year I got a school report which indicated that I'd become over-confident, and that there should be an immediate curtailment of my theatrical activities. I had to go and see the headmaster — when people got especially bad reports, they were carpeted, and had an interview with the ultimate authority — I was told in most severe terms that I had to concentrate on my academic studies — that is, I was to get down to the serious business of preparing myself for what life was to be all about.

'But I still went to the theatre. I saw *The Alchemist, Under Milk Wood, Twelfth Night,* plays by Ibsen, Molière — an excellent production of *The Queen and the Rebels,* by Ugo Betti. I remember Peter Coe did a fine version of *Henry IV, Part 1.* There was a totally bare stage with a table, a couple of stools and a large wooden chair; the entire production was done with just those pieces and lighting, and that was a complete revelation, that the theatre could make such imaginative demands. I was very fortunate because the grammar school I attended did have an excellent English department, headed by a man called Peter Hewett. He was besotted with the theatre, and promoted the putting on of plays whenever he could. I still cannot account for why he was a schoolteacher at a grammar school and hadn't years before decided to make his living in the theatre or as a novelist. He did everything from Shakespeare productions to the end-of-term reviews. There was a constant theatre output in the school. I adored him; I idolized him.

'Probably those two influences of the Ipswich Theatre and my English master meant that when I left school I was absolutely clear that there was only one profession that I was going to have anything to do with; if it would have anything to do with me.

'I went to Cambridge (on a scholarship). I came from a home where I couldn't possibly go to Cambridge to take a week of open scholarship exams without some kind of subsidy. My father was a cabinet-maker — well, he still is, and money was very scarce. There was a fund at the school to cover such extremities (called the poor boys' fund) and so I had to ask permission from that same headmaster — which was refused. It was only at the intervention of Peter Hewett that I was allowed to take the examination, and fortunately got an Open Exhibition.

'While I was at university I was involved in thirty-two productions — it was like weekly rep there. I didn't actually direct them all myself but I was either the assistant director or director or I was playing a leading part. The standard was very, very high. There were university actors there who were pitted, pocked and mature and looked fifty years of age. There were no problems about casting your heavy old, your Falstaffs and Lears. I suppose it was the influence of National Service which was just coming to an end, and which I was thankfully spared. There were people there like Derek Jacobi, Terry Hardiman, Julian Curry, Ian McKellen, Richard Cotterell, David Frost was turning in the occasional performance, Peter Cook was still acting in plays from time to time, and while I was there more turned up, like John Shrapnel and Richard Eyre and then that amazing bunch, John Cleese, Graham Chapman and most of the Monty Python cast. Corin Redgrave was there; he was not only a leading actor but *the* director of the period — everyone looked to his authority. John Barton had just left the scene to go to Stratford, though of course George Rylands was still there running the Marlowe

Society.

'We had our own theatre, the ADC Theatre, which was controlled by a committee of undergraduates. It was our responsibility to find productions for the theatre, to run it at a profit and organize teams of stage management and house management, to look after it for fifty-two weeks of the year. What better training could there possibly be for young people wishing to get into the professional theatre? It seemed to us who worked in it totally adult, the real thing. We used not only to get notices in the national Press, but to expect them. I got more reviews for any productions at Cambridge than I did in my first two years in the professional theatre. We did tours. I did a production of *Macbeth* — and we played at the Moss Empire Theatre in Newcastle. A bunch of students played this tragedy in a 3 000-seater variety house. In my last year we took a company (for the first time) to the Edinburgh Festival and did three productions and opened a night club. We adapted an old house, knocked a couple of rooms together and built a small auditorium. Then next year we sold it to another group which called itself the Traverse. History.

'By the time I left Cambridge I had no other qualifications except for work in the theatre. I mean, I got a degree. I scraped up my statutory second. While I was in Edinburgh, Anthony Richardson, who was then at Coventry, offered me a job as his assistant on a new play by David Turner, and shortly after that I was awarded one of those ABC TV director's scholarships and was told I could continue at Coventry. So there I was, Coventry being only fifteen miles away from the scene where it was all happening, Stratford-upon-Avon. I was very fortunate that certain things that I did at Coventry got seen by people from the RSC, and eventually I was asked if I'd go there as an assistant director.

'The first production I did at Coventry was *The Keep* by Gwyn Thomas, and my first leading actor was — David Waller — who was about to go into an enforced retirement, and was contemplating running a travel agency. I never did any Shakespeare, though. I was deeply disappointed. I was there for two years, and I thought at one stage I was going to do *Twelfth Night,* but I wasn't allowed to.

'Even at Stratford I didn't do Shakespeare for a long time. The first major thing I did for the RSC was *The Revenger's Tragedy*. During that year '66 Peter Hall had been forced into a policy of cutback and revival, which I have been faced with a number of times since. The position with the Arts Council was bad, we had absolutely no money, it looked as if we would have to pull out of London. So Peter tried a last desperate throw, to keep as much of the existing company together as possible. We churned out *Henry IV*, Parts 1 and 2, *Hamlet, Henry V,* previously successful productions, but for the *third* time running, and we were only able to do one new production with a very small cast and a very low budget. Towards the end of the year Peter said we're going to *have* to do one other thing and it's about time you did one, what would you like to do? Brood. *The Revenger's Tragedy* was a play I'd read a number of times for academic reasons at Cambridge, and I'd been absolutely knocked out by it. I thought it was one of the great undiscovered or at least unperformed plays, so I suggested it and Peter said, the problem is going to be expense, I just don't think you're going to be able to do something demanding luxurious richness with the resources we've got. I thought about it again and said to him it would be perfectly possible to do it inside his *Hamlet* set, so the bargain was struck. I brought in Chris Morley, who I'd worked with at Coventry, and he performed an amazing transformation on John Bury's original design.'

But at that stage he had no idea that he would be taking over from Peter Hall. 'I had no idea even the day before. I was flabbergasted. My first reaction was to want to change Peter's mind about resigning. I kept thinking if only he could be persuaded to go away for a sabbatical someone could take over for a short time; he might be sufficiently refreshed to be able to pick up the reins again. That's all I could say to him to begin with — "Please don't go." It was like the break-up of a marriage after a long period; the company never contemplated the possibility of Peter "leaving home". The organisation was not the least bit prepared for his departure. It was his creation, and it relied totally on his personal veto or sanction for everything that ever occurred in its name. Peter used to refer to the organization as a benevolent dictatorship, and although it was

a joke, it was also true. When my appointment was announced
Peter and I stressed the importance of continuity, but it was
nevertheless a great shock to the system. I had only just
learned to run a rehearsal, let alone a company. Following
Peter Hall was like being a comedian at the Windmill, the
really exciting thing had just disappeared. I can't always escape
the feeling that people are waiting for the *next* really exciting
thing to appear. It's hardly surprising. Peter Hall is the most
extraordinary man I know of who has ever devoted his talents
to running a theatre company.

'I was deeply influenced by him. I suppose from time to
time I require a completely idolatrous relationship in my life.
Peter Hewett was the first and Peter Hall was the second. He is
a man of such varied, even contradictory, talents, he's a
complete man, one part of him is the Machiavel, the politician,
negotiator, strategist and manipulator, another part is
vulnerable and passionate, the isolated artist, another part is
generous and familial, he is a bad actor and a very funny
mimic, he is formidable and a softy, a good writer, a pianist,
a fisherman, a naturalist and an interior decorator of startling
originality. He is also like me a Suffolk boy, although he
fights against his Puritanism more successfully.

'I think my own work with the RSC has fallen into two
clear categories. The work that I have had time to do and the
work I haven't. Before I had anything to do with running the
company there was a carefree sufficiency in my life, or so I
like to think. I did two or three productions in a year, with
long preparation and gestation periods which are so necessary
for really good work. It's so vital for a director to have the
time not only to read but to live a bit, observe, partake, be
part of the human race. It's wonderful but also necessary to
let a play hang around inside you for a month or so before
you start to articulate any thoughts about it. I found certain
images would keep returning, images which couldn't be
shaken off. They might be very perverse to begin with and
yet they would continue to restate themselves in slightly
different forms over a period of time. Gradually I would
come to the point of commitment to do a play and forming
an idea of how it should be cast, and therefore how it should
be rehearsed — frenetically or gently, collectively or individu-

ally and so on.

'I found all that totally engrossing. I found no lack in my life. Well, the number of times that I've been able to do that over the past four years is exactly nil, because the Aldwych and the desk at Stratford, claim 80 per cent of my time; which isn't to say I don't have some very talented and loyal people to work alongside me, because I do, but still the claim on my time, the claim on my nerves, the claim even on the thinking that goes on in my sleep, is 80 per cent concerned with the administration of this megalith.

'The productions I do these days are attempting to fit in with other priorities. I was lucky in the case of *The Winter's Tale*. It just so happened that I had a month in Stratford with very little else to work on except the play. Also Terry Hands was doing a production of *Pericles* at the same time, and I'd agreed that he should have first call on the greater bulk of the company during the opening rehearsal period and therefore I concentrated on Judi Dench, Barrie Ingham, Dickie Pasco, Nick Selby and Brenda Bruce; it was really that small group who "found" the play and became very committed to a certain way of expressing it. You can't fake discoveries in this business, and we all knew very early on that a very intractable play was opening up. We were in touch with it. Our sense of discovery made us use our theatre in a new way — new to us — a big white void, a free-ranging use of the space defined only by the actors use of it, a celebration of what was consciously allegoric in the play and not an uncomfortable naturalistically localized series of symbolic nudges. I was interested too in all those songs in the famous, or notorious, pastoral act. That section just became a musical, and for the first time I felt completely free of any strictures about form and period and fidelity — we were on to that play, and we *needed* every syllable Shakespeare had given us to communicate it.

'In contrast at the end of that season I did a production of *Henry VIII,* and I am ashamed to admit it, but I only had five days' preparation and found myself talking to a company of thirty-five actors, knowing very little more about the play than they did, and trying to plan the thing and plot it out as we went along, even designing the set with John Bury as we went along. That should never happen in a theatre company that is attempting to do Shakespeare better than anybody else — because Shakespeare (or Beaumont and Fletcher for that matter) won't play ball. I think certain minimum conditions are vital, and to put it bluntly I haven't been giving myself these conditions for too long.

'Even with *Hamlet,* it was a curiously beleaguered production — many things were claiming my attention at the London end, a new third auditorium season, for instance, the season we did at the Round House. I was trying to organize that, and therefore my attention was very split, which is not to say I didn't enjoy much of that planning work, nor indeed many of the *Hamlet* rehearsals. I think I'm rapidly approaching the moment when I'm going to want to do *Hamlet* again, because the *Hamlet* I did with Alan Howard was really an exercise for both of us, but a very valuable exercise for all that. What I tried to do, mistakenly, was a production which had five different intentions. This was quite conscious, and certain interesting things emerged. The examination of *Hamlet's* madness was central. Alan and I arrived at the certainty that Hamlet does become mad and after the play scene is no longer playing games. His mind actually turns, and he is no longer responsible for his own actions. The murder of Polonius is the action of someone who really doesn't know what he's doing. It's obsessive, possessed, Hamlet is getting something demonic out of his system. We were intrigued and disturbed by it. We were trying to present a world shocked by ninety-nine good Lutheran *reasons* why nothing was *absolute* any more, and we placed in Claudius's study a first crudely modelled spherical globe. Right and wrong, heaven and hell, in an advancing age of reason was just more than one Wittenberg student could cope with. "There are more things in heaven and earth, Horatio, than are dreamt of in your philosophy." We tried to suggest that the leaving of Elsinore for England was some kind of purgative or cleansing for Hamlet, even though there are people are as mad as he. In his absence somebody else goes *really* mad, Ophelia.

'We also tried to approach the play through the metaphor of the players (is Hamlet playing at madness or really mad?).

In an otherwise monochromatic presentation of the play, we had this one outburst of colour and travel-stained grime in the players' costumes, the instructions to the players took on a more ironic quality than I have previously known — and the sequence finished with Hamlet robing himself in the only black costume the players possessed, a monk's garb, before the melodrama of "Now might I do it pat," and the visit to his mother which so frightens her.'

And how does he now feel about his concept of the true ensemble company to which he gave so much time and thought? Does he still feel the same? 'No, I don't. I continue to want it to work. I don't think the concept has yet worked anywhere in England, apart perhaps from small studio groups, or companies that have certain shared political beliefs, but who work in unsubsidized opposition to the present establishment. I think the failure has got a great deal to do with the prevailing conditions in our whole profession. British actors have the advantage of a unique theatre tradition, and so feel in touch with and slightly responsible to the highest ideals and intentions of European companies. But they also have the English language, which is Hollywood, and world success language, so they are drawn equally to the free-enterprise personality-orientated American flesh markets, to get rich quick, or at the very least, to get rich.

'But look what has happened to the British film industry, or what has happened in television. There is less work, and so paradoxically there is a reluctance of actors to commit themselves for long periods, there is an increasing unpopularity in the notion of the long-term contract. I think the problem with the RSC is that we are two companies and we try constantly to develop two ensembles, which is asking the impossible, especially when we can quite clearly see that nobody has as yet successfully developed one. But then, when the RSC was first formulated, the fact that an attempt was being made to forge a company was exciting; now the fact is a commonplace, and everybody is left to contemplate the relative failure of the attempt.

'I don't believe in equality; it's clear that there are certain actors who are more capable of playing leading parts than others, and it will always be so. An actor is not a bad or a

doomed actor if he hasn't the charisma to play one of
Shakespeare's most demanding, leading parts. Excellent
supporting actors are very necessary to the idea of an
ensemble. But I do think, for an ensemble to work, it has
first of all to be smaller than any group we are currently
employing. It has to be higher-paid, and so economically
more attractive to the higher quality of actor. It has to
commit itself in advance for a number of years, and it has to
play a very large part in the decision-making which is going
to determine its own future. Most of all, it has to believe in
the possibility of becoming the most skilled, expert, highly
trained flexible troupe performing the works of Shakespeare
to be found in the world.

'At present in the RSC almost everything that we do is
finally determined by money; the perimeters within which
we work are scarifyingly narrow. If we miscalculate on a
year's work by 5 per cent we would be close to extinction.
Our turnover is rapidly approaching two million pounds a
year. I cannot afford to take decisions which can only be
justified artistically if they're going to lead to the loss of a
quarter of a million pounds. However, if I am committed to
creating a genuine ensemble I might have to take such
decisions. For too long the RSC has been a place of compromise. I don't think we've ever lost sight of our ideals, or
done productions for the wrong reasons, we've never done
any exploitation of our work solely for commercial reasons,
but we have to recognize that all of our choices are influenced
by our precarious economics.'

In 1972-3 he took on his biggest project, that of directing
all four of Shakespeare's Roman plays. 'I took one year off
from directing any other plays in order to give myself the
time to prepare for it, but of course it didn't work out that
way. I spent the time reorganizing our workshops and technical
services.' He enjoyed the initial rehearsal period. 'We had a
bare, empty space in Floral Street, in Covent Garden. We
worked long hours throughout the day, and went on to
sessions in the evening. The interchange of ideas then, the
improvizational work that we did, the exercises and experiments, the work on verse, on voice, on bodies, the physical
creation of a company by promoting a greater and greater

dependence of those actors on each other, contributed to one
of the most rewarding periods of rehearsal I've ever experienced. I think those first six weeks produced a loyalty to the
project that never wavered, and the actors had to take a lot
of very hard knocks over the two years.

'There was a holding back from some critics who thought
the four plays shouldn't have been done together. I said
repeatedly that they did not amount to a cycle, but that
didn't alter the assumption of many critics that I was
presenting a Roman *Wars of the Roses* or *Forsyte Saga*. I
wanted to do all four plays in the same season to find out
what relationship they *do* have to each other. I think we
discovered they have more than anybody first thought.

'There were fierce criticisms of the new hydraulically
operated stage. I think I used it overmuch in the first production, though less in *Julius Caesar,* and not at all in *Titus*. I
think I was to some degree fascinated by a technological
marvel. On the other hand, I'm certain it points a way forward, and many more designers and directors are going to
want to use that kind of equipment. Whatever else, it's an
incredible boon for us because it helps with all our change-
over problems, and we can provide ourselves with different
rakes.

'I think it marks the climax of a certain development of
design for us. Chris Morley and I have been working very hard
at trying to find a way of presenting Shakespeare in a permanent chamber, and the grey box (*King Lear*) and white box
(*Winter's Tale*) seasons were expressions of this aesthetic. But
the relationship of stage to auditorium at Stratford is bad —
the actor feels very isolated. We have also proposed that the
stage is a platform merely, filling one end of a large room,
which is the auditorium. The attempts on our part to
encourage the audience not to expect naturalistic design
solutions to provoke the imagination and to make the language
the most vital part of the experience, led to the design of a
number of sets that were perhaps too stereotyped. The
chambers in which we did *Pericles*, the *Winter's Tale, Measure
for Measure, Richard III* and *Hamlet* were just a little bit too
similar. What Chris and I were trying to do with the hydraulic
device was to make something which could be a chamber,

walled, roofed and enclosed, and which could be a totally
open platform or anything between those two extremes. We
provided for an upper stage, an inner stage, steps, all of
which could disappear, or build themselves in ten seconds.
All of that came out of one season's production costs, which
was miraculous. These facilities now exist for whoever wants
to use them.

'In the near future I shall have to take some very bold
decisions. If the company is to survive at all we must reassess
and restate our priorities. Shakespeare wrote for a non-visual
theatre. All his plays were written to be presented within an
unchanging permanent structure. We don't know exactly
what it looked like, but we do know it was *permanent.* We
know the budgetary concentration of those Elizabethan
companies was on their costumes; on how splendid the actor
looked.

'Apart from costume, visual presentation was probably
minimal. Therefore Shakespeare's audience went to the
theatre *knowing* it was to see a permanent stage, with
permanent doorways, balconies, windows, so it was able to
concentrate immediately on the expression of character and
relationship through language, not on stage pictures. Towards
the end of Shakespeare's lifetime a new theatre, the masque
theatre, was starting to develop, indoors, artifically lit,
lavishly expensive. Read the words of most masques written
at the time; they *stink*; Shakespeare's was a *language* theatre.
He was responding to begin with to the prevailing conditions
governing expression, and his plays continually celebrate the
magical transforming power of the actor. Nothing up his
sleeve, the actor presents the word to the audience, and this
breaks down all barriers between people because actor and
audience have joined together in a collective art of imagination. As the chorus in *Henry V* says, "On your imaginary
forces work." Peter Brook's production of *A Midsummer
Night's Dream* was a thrilling expression of this celebration.

'It seems to me that in *The Tempest* Shakespeare is very
sensitive to the new competitive masque theatre. So he
presents his bare island with his allegoric people, his airy
spirit, his earthy monster, his exiled philosopher, his younger
generation and he says, "The Masque theatre is a dead form";

he *provides* a masque in all its visual richness and lavishness
and its statutory paucity of language, and abruptly interrupts
it for no reason at all. Prospero then speaks about that masque
in language which is so much more visual, evocative, translucent
and shimmering then anything that could have appeared in
the masque itself. Shakespeare seems to be saying that the
masque is *not* what the theatre is about, and if we are to
believe this is Shakespeare's valedictory, then it contains a
warning to all who are to come after. Over the years since
*The Tempest* the theatre has gone through endless cycles of
getting its priorities totally wrong.

'The RSC can still be accused of being a kind of opera
house. Audiences still assemble wondering what new visual
splendour is going to appear. It seems to me that we've got to
get back to the point where an audience knows that it's going
to arrive at a place where there'll be a structure they like and
feel comfortable with, which doesn't impose on them, and
then on to that structure come actors who achieve by their
expertise, their skill, and of course their passion, the
necessary suspension of our collective disbelief. I don't
mean one should be consciously archaic and attempt to
reconstruct the Globe, but the notion of a permanent space,
where plays are performed, is vital, for only in that way are
we going to reaffirm our priorities in terms of a concentration
on the actors, a concentration upon the language, and a concentration upon the imagination of the audience. We must
stop dissipating our time, energy and money on long technical
periods to create illusion. The RSC has got to spend its
money from now on on the sheer excellence, the unsurpassed
excellence, of the performance of the plays of Shakespeare
by superbly accomplished actors.

'Over the last two years the price rises in the materials that
we use most have been 100 per cent. This means that if we
continue to work in the way we are at the moment we're
going to be able to buy less and less, and so our standards will
sink lower and lower, unless we make our seat prices higher
and higher. Which raises the whole question of what subsidy
is for, and who we are playing to. I would like our seat prices
to come down. I would like much cheaper seats for kids and
students. I would like a certain number of free performances

each year. The RSC has got to reach more to the Midlands community, and eventually to the City and East End community around the Barbican. I dislike the feeling that each year we play to a million passers-by.

'The most difficult task for a designer is to organize space, to work brilliantly and evocatively with nothing. I think our designers have been getting more expert in this, but since in the future nothing is all we can afford they have to get even better. The true relationship that must exist during the performance of a play is between the dramatist and the audience, through the actors. For too long it has been between the director/designer and the critics. Interpretation — "I see this play as" — that's the unimportant top layer of a production.

'I think the most exhausting and exciting thing about the RSC is that every day of our lives we're measuring ourselves against the greatest tragedies and comedies that have been written. There's never a moment when we're not tackling one of them. Other companies can let their hair down a bit, do something off-beat and then build up their resources to tackle one great play. We have to do all the great plays once every five years. There are only thirty-seven plays in the canon; if we're performing our function at all we must be presenting most of them, and since we're tackling them in the expectation of being the best, of course we fail, over and over again.

'On the other hand, we do occasionally, succeed. My list of successes is short and personal. Peter Hall's *The Wars of the Roses,* and *Hamlet,* the Brook *Lear* and *Dream,* I think probably my *Revenger's Tragedy* and the *Winter's Tale,* Terry Hands's *Merry Wives of Windsor,* John Barton's *Twelfth Night, All's Well, Troilus and Cressida* and *Richard II.* It's probably too early to judge, but I think I won't be ashamed of *Julius Caesar* at Stratford and *Coriolanus* and *Antony and Cleopatra* in London.'

Looked at in that overall expectation of excellence, it does not seem a bad proportion.

# Robin Phillips

The first time I met Robin Phillips he was up to his neck in
trouble before the opening of *Two Gentlemen of Verona* at
Stratford-on-Avon. Just before the opening night, the powers
that be had decided his unusual production would not work.
He stood firm. The atmosphere in the theatre became too
fraught for words, and I remember being collared by one of
the leading players who shot off a stream of abuse at those
who didn't have any faith in the production and ended 'Put
that on your front page', only to ring me, feverishly, in the
small hours of the morning and say he hoped I had not taken
him at his word.

Such emotional dramas are not usually associated with
Robin Phillips. The first production of his I remember was
*The Beggar's Opera* at the Northcott Theatre, Exeter,
followed by *A Midsummer Night's Dream*. (Another theatre
director said to me once when discussing Tony Church, the
first director of the Northcott, 'After all, he *invented* Robin
Philips'. He is above all an actors' director, and actors who
have worked with him in Exeter, Stratford, Chichester and
Greenwich all agree. No doubt in his new appointment as
director in Stratford, Ontario, the same will apply, perhaps
because he began his career in the theatre by doing more
acting than directing.

'In fact, I trained as a director, a designer and an actor,
with the intention always of going into direction. Even at
seventeen I saw it was necessary to do the acting for a bit, so,
having trained for all three, one bided one's time until it
seemed ripe to change. But it wasn't really a switch, the
intention was there from the beginning. I don't mean I knew
I wanted to direct before I went to drama school but very
soon after I got there the man who was training me decided
I really ought to be a director, not an actor.

'It's difficult to say just what influenced me first. I know a very early and exciting thing was *The Power and the Glory* which Brook directed; probably not a very typical Brook piece of work. I don't know whether *he* would consider it typical, or if all the good Brook things were present in it, but I was terribly excited by it. It was the combination of Scofield and Brook that really began to thrill me. Other than that, there were all the usual things, schoolboy trips to the Old Vic and so on, that really got one intrigued by the theatre, but that Brook production was the first that got me *intrigued* specifically.

'But it's very rarely a director's work only that influences you, it's a combination of actor and director, because that's when a piece of work is at its most complete; the person there doing it is so much at one with the production. Then again, there's the relationship between a director and a certain writer and a designer. I mean Hall, Pinter and Bury *together* have given one an incredible amount of excitement and a fresh vitality about what one thinks of theatre. The marvellous thing about Brook, though, is the number of doors he's constantly opening. He opens vast doors and allows other people to pass through them and stumble into the field and sniff around.'

He tends to talk in terms of designing a production rather than directing it. 'The most difficult thing, always working in the kind of places where I've worked, is that I've never been free enough to design a production after we've rehearsed, which would be the best way of doing it, because of the economic necessity to have designs ready, approved and perhaps even started and being built before you begin rehearsals. The essential thing, by talking to the designer and the actors before you start, is to try and discover what the overall intention of the author is and you must try and find that intention because from it spreads the feeling of whether the play is attacking or embracing you. The ground-plan that the actors have to work on, and the environment they have to live in, stems from his intention. You have to decide whether a set should just quite openly stand square on to the audience or whether it should be more sly and oblique or whether you should feel the audience is drawn in and embraced by it.

'All that has to come from what the author is trying to say, what his basic intention is, and from that you discover how the play should be designed. As in a lot of Restoration plays, there's a flow of language that goes with a certain way of living, and you have to try and discover what that's likely to be. I mean, you need to know when people enter a stage whether they need to be automatically thrown into a curve, what's the natural way for them to move, whether when they come on they should come straight up against a table and have to move or turn at awkward angles and navigate the furniture. All this must be planned beforehand. At least, that's the way I work. You don't always have to if you're lucky enough to start rehearsing first and try it all kinds of different ways and then at a certain stage say, "Ah, now we're beginning to get it," and start to design it. That's the *best* way — but few of us have that opportunity or are able to make such decisions. Sometimes you find you've made the wrong ones, and you're left with a set which is aggressive, and you're in despair because you know the play isn't aggressive at all, it's gentle and loving. Then you really do have problems.

'But it's trying to find all that in the text to start off with that matters, not necessarily the moment-to-moment motiva-tion of the characters. It's a basis on which one feels the play stands, and then one relates that to the designer, and if one can discuss it with the actors too before one starts, they're aware of the way it's going to go.'

A number of the same people tend to turn up in his pro-ductions. 'Yes, some come from a long way back, the family grows all the time and you can draw on an ever-increasing pool. It is an advantage. It saves an awful lot of time, because you can use a sort of shorthand and can get down straight away to just what you want to do. The more I work with people the more I realize that the discovery area is the most important, and how close we can get towards feeling what it's about. All the same, you still have nerves, you're still frightened as to whether you're serving the play as you should, and actually communicating what you think. Those worries are always around.

'During the discovery period you can try all kinds of things.

I don't have movement classes as such here at Greenwich, partly because of economics, but we do work on the voice. You can't divorce voice from movement because it is movement in one sense, and has to do with the body in the same way, but we had a very interesting time for example when we did the Lorca, when we tried to find out how best we could give the impression of speaking a foreign language without actually using an accent. But time always limits how much you can achieve.

'That was what was so splendid about working for the Royal Shakespeare Company, you really did have time to work on voice and movement because there were people paid to teach it. Stratford was enormously valuable. It's a remarkable company when I think of it other than in terms of the "Two Gents", when what had been idyllic for seven weeks suddenly became absolute hell. They've got so many foundations there that it's marvellous to say "Oh, God, I don't have to build that," and you can start straight in with the work. Then it's so much easier financially, the resources of a company like that are just so splended and you don't have to say we can't do that because we can't afford it, but to know you can have absolutely what you want in order to express whatever it is the author wants to share with the audience. So often one has to say, "The ideal thing would be this", but it's too expensive. Like the trampoline in the World Theatre Season's *Yerma* that got all the notices. In fact we'd been meaning to use one in our Lorca too, but finally it had to go. There wasn't the time to get the actors used to it because they were rehearsing more than one play at once and it was too expensive to put in with three plays in repertoire. It's always sad when you have to shelve an exciting idea for those kind of reasons. I mean, I don't mind throwing out a thousand ideas while we work, but when it comes from a non-creative source, you can't because of censorship, you can't because of money, well that really hurts.'

When I first talked to him about the traumatic *Two Gentlemen* he was quite clear what he saw in the play. 'It's a play about love and friendship — and just how important friendship is once love becomes involved. It's about the

awful problems of adolescence — and they are awful. I set it
in a finishing school because I wanted to show these young
people emerging into adults — they had left school in every
sense. Valentine has obviously matured by the end; after all
he has just seen his best friend try to rape his girl friend.
Using the Beatles *All you need is love* at the end wasn't a
gimmick — for this is what it's all been about. They should
have realized that love is an essential. Whether they have or
not is an open question. They pair off at the end — it will be
all right, won't it? Or will it? You just don't know. Come
next week and see *Love's Labour's Lost* and see what happens.'

    Looking back on it now, he feels he got the general intention
right. 'When I was first asked to do it I thought, God, no,
because I'd never read it and when I'd seen it done it was always
in fey little Victorian versions, so I went off and read it, and I
was quite sure it wasn't like anything I'd seen done before. It's
not mature Shakespeare, the play doesn't hang together in
places, there are breaks in the plot. I think he had the plots
of *Romeo and Juliet, Comedy of Errors* and *Love's Labour's
Lost* all seething about in his head when he wrote it. But it
deals with extraordinary and powerful adolescent emotions.
It has an incredible depth, and the most remarkable thing
about it to me is the character of Launce, which is something
Shakespeare never does anywhere else, one just can't find
anywhere the sort of style he chooses for that character in a
prophetic sense. It has seeds and roots in people like Jaques,
but it's a unique style of writing he never used again. I find
that fascinating.'

    As well as Stratford he has directed a number of times at
Chichester, and this, he says, affected the way he works.
'John Clements has a very strong line as to what he wanted
his theatre to be. I don't mean the RSC don't, but within
their framework they give you enormous freedom and you
can pretty well have your head, but Sir John is very sure
about what his audience is — or was, when he was there —
and I had to work under a much tighter brief. If you couldn't
convince him about the way you wanted to do something then
you had the choice of either not doing it or doing it specifically as he wanted it to be done, in the style of the entertain-
ment he wanted for his theatre. I found this most valuable.

Twice very strong ideas of mine were vetoed, but I don't
regret deciding to work under his banner rather than saying,
"If I can't do it my way, thank you very much, goodbye." It
was more valuable to do it and see if one could still say what
one wanted to under those conditions.'

Asked what authors he enjoyed directing most, he turned
the question aside, and you can see why actors feel as they
do about him. 'It's the actors who are the more enjoyable
aspect for me. I've been very much tied to the classics
throughout my career, so although one is intrigued and
interested and fascinated by Strindberg, Ibsen or Lorca, it's
not the same as working on new plays with new authors, and
because of this classical emphasis the interest for me has as
much to do with, say, Joan Plowright in *Rosmersholm* rather
than just *Rosmersholm*. Ibsen is there too, of course, but
because there have been so many productions and one knows
them, the interest is much more to do with the play plus the
actor concerned. It's always a group activity and response;
you can't say this is *my* production of Ibsen, I just don't
have those sort of feelings about plays. It has to be Ibsen
with Plowright because so much of what one is doing has to
do with her personally. The Ibsen part is understood unless
you're doing somebody's variation on Ibsen. It's the combination of that person and what that person has got and
can discover in a play that another actor or actress couldn't.'

His year at Greenwich has taken in all kinds of plays. 'We
have a very discerning audience. Very mixed and responsive,
but if they decide not to come then they just don't come.'
His final production was *Zorba the Greek*. 'The theatre had
been a music hall and I wanted to continue its constant link
with the musical world. *Zorba*'s an extraordinary piece in
lots of funny, subtle little ways. It's also a powerful story,
and it's fascinating the way a stage play has been arrived at.
Instead of a Greek chorus, it's a musical-comedy Greek
chorus. I don't mean they all stand in lines wearing masks
and wailing and going up and down on stilts and so on, but
it has a strange, strange atmosphere. The author's an
incredible man. When he wrote the novel he said, "I've been
a Christian, a Buddhist, I've been whatever", and he talks
about various philosophies and religions. "Then there is

Zorba," he says after mentioning Christ. He does have a
unique philosophy, very interesting and powerful; not
neccessarily what we all believe, but it's difficult not
to because he really *does;* for it has generosity, warmth
and love of life. He says, in fact, that the only death
that is really bad is the death you die by not living life every
minute. Death from revenge, death from war, these things
are inevitable, they come to us all. We die in our beds or
we're shot — that's just death. But the unforgivable one is
the one where you die sitting in your chair because you
won't get up and do anything. That's important. Nowadays
one looks around and there are endless strikes and problems
and wailing and moaning and one wonders where the zest
just for living has gone. I mean there've always been rich
people, better off than others, and those others worrying
about their positions, and one just wonders how much happier
those with the money are. I come from a real working-class
background, and the simplicity of that upbringing and the
honesty and directness that I gained from my parents is more
valuable than anything *untold* wealth can buy. My mother
was in domestic service all her life, and my father a gardener.
It not only kept my feet on the ground, but well and truly
planted. The simple truths of what makes a garden grow are
also what makes a healthy work. I owe these generous, honest,
human beings more than anything I can ever repay. I think
that one's searching in whatever one does for that background
they gave me, and you just can't have the right sort of
generosity of spirit in any other. I'm convinced that somewhere along the line I've been very fortunate by being made
aware of what true values are. I don't meant that this is the
only way — just that for me it's been very fortunate.'

Sadly, he is leaving this country to take up his appointment
in Canada. 'My ambition is to have a company of my own,'
he said at the end of my first interview with him in 1970. His
is a rare talent, and we have not got enough in this country
to spare, so why will he go? 'Need — I work best when I'm
needed. Not just because it's a dolly job, I mean, if I'd wanted
the splendours I wouldn't have spent a year in Greenwich; it's
been a hard grind with no money and a lot of work.' He will
have three theatres, the main one of which was used as a

basis for Chichester, 'though it appears — having seen Stratford, Ont. — that Chichester was designed by somebody just tipping up a dustbin and deciding how exciting that looked, and doing it. It's utterly unlike Stratford, which is the most exciting theatre I've ever been in. It's wonderful, it *demands* people. As you walk into the auditorium the stage is empty, demanding that people should talk on it. Incredible!' 1974 has been spent planning his first major season, using all three auditoria, which will be in 1975. 'The most interesting part will be discovering Canadian playwrights.' He was chosen from directors from all over the world. 'I don't know why they chose me. I hope they were right.'

# Clifford Williams

The first time I talked to Clifford Williams was when he was in the middle of rehearsing *The Duchess of Malfi* at Stratford-on-Avon and had just come back from putting on *Oh! Calcutta!* in Paris. Whatever I expected of the director who chose the first (which has for me the most chilling lines in any play, when the Cardinal says, looking into his fishponds, 'Methinks I see a thing armed with a rake, that seems to strike at me') and then became the centre of controversy over the second, I really did not know, but certainly I expected someone a great deal more aggressive and didactic, and this he certainly is not.

His progression to directing is more unusual than most, and no doubt this is why he shows such a varied range.

'I don't know quite why I decided to be a director but I can certainly remember when. I was at school and about the age of fourteen or fifteen and for some curious reason I had taken to reading poetry, especially the poetry of W.B. Yeats. I'd only just become aware of poetry, and it was an esoteric choice but somehow or other it appealed to me. I wasn't a particularly literary inclined chap but I felt fairly intensely. Yeats had written some plays, *Four Plays for Dancers,* and it probably seemed a curious choice at that time, but I decided quite soon that I wanted to do one of these plays, and also wanted very much to act in it. So I got a production together with people at school.

'I hadn't acted much at school — it was a fairly average grammar school — and we didn't go in for that sort of thing much, but we managed to get a group of chaps together and I hired the local library and put on *The Dreaming of the Bones* and sold tickets, in the happy and gullible belief that the massed ranks of the general public would flock to Islington to see a few boys in a play by W.B. Yeats. To my astonishment some forty or fifty people did turn up, enough

at least for us to break even without expenses. So it was
through Yeats that I found my interest in the theatre.
Anyway, inspired by our success, we thought we'd put on
another production, and this time we gave excerpts from
*Macbeth* which was no doubt *ghastly*. I can't think what we
could possibly have been up to. I was about fifteen by this
time and had discovered Gordon Graig. How I heard about
him I don't know. Possibly through Yeats again, because he
must have been connected with Yeats, as he did designs for
some of his plays. I remember being most excited over his
idea of space being relative — for instance, if you put a spot
on a postage stamp the spot seems minute and the stamp
seems large, even though the stamp itself is small. I was
overwhelmed by this, and had lots of pieces of scenery
throwing heavy shadows. We also discovered that we could
encourage local girls to act with us.

'Perhaps I only had an interest in theatre at all because of
the girls . . . . That was when it all began to go wrong,
because the librarian discovered a group of boys and girls up
on the roof. I was never quite sure what they were up to, I
imagine it was fairly innocent, but I was hauled over the
coals and told I couldn't put my plays on again if this was
going to happen. I undertook that it wouldn't, but in about
a day the boys and girls were back up on the roof, and that
was it. I felt I'd been most unfairly treated in having to stop
my productions and the work I was doing because of a silly
rule, so I dropped the whole thing, I thought for good, at
the age of fifteen.

'I spent the next two years studying economics and aiming
to go to university. Then one day I just got fed up with it all
and decided to drop it. I went along to the Embassy Theatre
in Swiss Cottage, which is now the Central School for Speech
and Drama, and they were just reopening with *Quality Street,*
which had a cast of Linden Travers, Jean Forbes-Robertson
and Geoffrey Toone. I asked if there were any jobs going and
they gave me one as a dresser to Geoffrey Toone. He seemed
to me to be an enormously tall and impressive chap. I was
overwhelmed with the whole experience, the heat, the makeup, because I hadn't been used to anything like that before.
I was frightened. All the actors seemed to be bigger, better,

more flesh and blood and have more spittle on their lips, than anyone I'd met before, so I was very impressed. I worked for the princely sum of 30s. a week, augmented by tips. Unfortunately, Jean Forbes-Robertson drank a great deal and she'd send me out to buy two or three double whiskies every night, and as she forgot to pay for these herself I had to pay for them out of my 30s. and I actually ended up out of pocket and having to draw on my meagre savings to keep going. Eventually I was very broke. I was already lying at home because I didn't dare tell my mother how badly I was paid. She was a widow and had struggled away there in Cardiff to make sure I could go to university.

'After this was over I went to the Chanticleer Theatre (which is now the Webber Douglas School). There were some interesting people there, Laurence Payne, Sheila Burrell, Joy Harvey and Freddie Valk who gave that incredible and unusual *Othello* back in '42. We did some interesting plays, a group of Ibsen, I remember another of Oststrovsky. I was a student or an assistant-assistant-assistant stage manager, a concept we no longer have in the theatre, where if you wanted to employ extras cheaply you got in a lot of people and called them students and paid them £1 a head. While I was there an unbelievably precocious chap came along full of his prowess at Oxford with a tremendous reputation, and he directed Cocteau's *Infernal Machine.* His name was Peter Brook, and he was the young lion, the *enfant terrible* of the Chanticleer. I wonder if he remembers now that *The Infernal Machine* was his first London production? I didn't guess at the time what was going to be his subsequent career.

'After this I was out of work again, and one day I met a friend of mine who said, "Come along, there's a good job going if you can do some mime." I had done some mime because of the Yeats/Gordon Craig period. On the appointed day a large lady bore down on us — Letty Littlewood — while hanging around in the background were some rather cold-looking, pretty girls. "Are you *strong*?" asked the lady briskly, "Would you lift this girl up, please? Will you put her down again, thank you." My friend, who was very camp, collapsed trying to lift his girl over his head, but I was told I'd managed to lift my girl *very well,* and that was how I

came to make my debut as a ballet dancer in the Anglo-
Russian ballet . . . .

'In fact my first part was in *Les Sylphides,* where there is
only one man. But there were so few male dancers around
that all Miss L. was interested in was whether I could actually
lift the girls off the ground. I became totally enamoured of
dancing, though I came to it much too late. I had great
hammer feet and a large arse but I was bitten by the whole
thing, grotesque as I must have been. But it did give me a
love of movement I might never have had if I hadn't had this
period of dance. Although I was too old for ballet, I discovered I could do modern dance. (The trouble with classical
ballet was that I couldn't "turn out".)

'About this time I fell in love with a ballet dancer — I was
all of nineteen — and then I got called up. Because I was a
pacifist I went along to the tribunal to register as a CO.
Before the tribunal I kept trying to argue what I felt about
violence and they kept saying, "You're a liar", and this went
on and on and we went through all the bit about what would
you do if you saw a German bayoneting your mother. I said,
"I don't know," and that wasn't the right answer. Anyway,
at that time they did give you an option, you could go down
the mines, so as I'm a Welshman and lived among miners I
decided I'd go down the mines and become a coal-miner. I
went down on the condition I could go off on Saturdays
from coal-mining to a ballet class. The parents of the ballet
dancer had been encouraging her to jilt me and about this
time she did it, and that really fucked things up. I'd lost out
in every way. I worked down the mine for eighteen months,
still going to ballet classes — not everybody goes straight
from pit boots to ballet shoes. You could change your mind
then and come out of the mines, so as the War ended,
although I was convinced of my own pacifism, I joined the
Army, which was unfortunate because I had to do my full
Army time on top of the eighteen months I'd done in the
mines.

'Later I was commissioned and found myself in Shropshire
doing Garrison Theatre, and somewhere there's a perfectly
ghastly photograph of me in tights with an ATS girl perched
on one shoulder, and the caption underneath says "the dancing

lieutenant". I was the rave of the *Salop Advertiser*. Afterwards
I did a little dancing, but I was little use after all that time
away, though I did once partner Markova; she was a little bit
of steel and had terrible language but it's something to say
you've done that.

'Finally I decided to do the job properly and went up to
Perth and did some serious work in rep. It was very good for
me because we toured the whole of Scotland from the
Shetland Islands to Edinburgh. From there I went to the
People's Palace in the Mile End Road — that was pre Joan
Littlewood. The company was full of film stars like Nigel
Patrick and I remember us doing a play which caused a
furore because it just mentioned Royalty sitting up in heaven
after they were dead. It seems tame now. I mention this
time because here I met John Roberts, who was going to have
a great influence on me later on. Then I formed my own
mime company because I was still involved with mime, the
dance thing and some kinky sidelines. We never had more than
six players, but we made forty or fifty mime plays which we
took out and toured all over the country. I put them together
through a mixture of research, inspiration and experiment.
We had very little money, we were always broke, though we
covered the country from the Scilly Isles to the Shetlands
(yet again). One of the good things was that we did some
work with deaf children, and my interest has remained and
I'm now on the committee for the National Theatre of the
Deaf and still teach and work with deaf children.

'I was always going to the Arts Council with hands out-
stretched. I only needed £250 per annum, but they said they
had no money for people who only did work for children
and schools. A statement I now find ironic when I see how
money is shovelled into projects of this kind. Perhaps if we'd
had our grant we would have still been going.

'Then I met David Scase and went to the Theatre Workshop
and met a whole lot of people with whom I've been associated
ever since, like Ewan MacColl, who was marrried to Joan
Littlewood. It was Joan Littlewood's first company, and from
there I went to John English's Arena Theatre, where I
actually began to direct. I took to directing because I'm
fundamentally lazy, I don't like having to go to the theatre

every evening.'

From the Arena he went to Africa as a drama examiner and found himself enough work to keep him there for three years, 'and I directed an all-black *Macbeth* in Entebbe, years before the Zulu one which came over here. I began directing in this country, at Canterbury, Hornchurch, and at the Arts Theatre where I did a whole mass of work, a weird selection of stuff, Lorca's *Yerma*, Dürrenmatt, O'Neill's *A Moon for the Misbegotten,* in which there was a young author called Colin Blakeley. I suppose you can say I fiddled around. I thought, God, I'm thirty-four and I haven't really done anything. I earned around seven pounds a week at the Arts Theatre and my marriage broke up about this time. I'd married one of the poor mime actresses who'd just had enough and took-off.

'Then John Roberts turned up again as London manager of the RSC and he offered me a job as a kind of staff rep producer who would come along and overlook the company and keep them up to scratch. I really found it a bit painful. I went along to see Peter Hall and told him I did feel I'd established and made a name for myself and it was a second-rate job, but he said "We'll pay you eighteen pounds a week," so I said "Yes, I'll take it." But, I fancy, he was very un-impressed with me, in fact he qas quite funny, he said, "Yes, we-ell, you can come in but you'll never be a producer here." He kept stressing they didn't use outside people, there was no room. In fact this situation has obtained to this day, and I don't think it's a particularly good one. People stay on the outside until some blinding chance comes along and they do a job and you pass immediately into the inner circle and you're inside and everything's all right after that. But it's a dangerous situation because you have virtually a closed shop. I don't know why they do it. Possibly just through fear. Peter Wood was going to direct *Afore Night Come* for them and then that miracle, that marvellous thing, happened. Just before he was about to start rehearsals he found he couldn't, and I was asked to do it, in a very grudging way. Then the following day Peter Hall said he'd changed his mind and this happened three times in all in the course of a week and in the end I said I'd too much pride to carry on like that and they could stuff their play. In the end I did do it.

Then lo and behold it happened again; Scofield's *Lear* was postoned and I did a hurried *Comedy of Errors*. After that I was accepted as an assistant director.'

In recent years he has been associated with two highly controversial productions, *Soldiers* and *Oh! Calcutta!* He had been directing in Canada as a guest director for some time with Theatre Toronto, but this had its problems. 'I had not researched the subject very deeply, and I hadn't realized that Canadian actors are very complicated indeed — they're well known for welcoming you with open arms and then shoving the dagger in the left shoulder-blade. That was a *bad* experience — we did some good work, but it was a bad experience. But during the period I was there I heard that Tynan was in trouble at the National over Hochhuth's *Soldiers*. I wrote to him saying I wanted to do the play in Toronto, and at first he wouldn't hear of it, but when it turned out that he wasn't going to get it for the National, I had it for Toronto. It was also interesting to see what kind of a reception it would have outside England, and what sort of problems it would throw up.

'So finally, after paying a lot of money, I did it there. It was unbelievable. Toronto's quite a big city, but it's a provincial one. Suddenly that event electrified the city — everyone started flying in, Rolf, Tynan, everyone you could think of. It was a fantastic success. I don't know why the Canadians should be so interested in Churchill, but they were all fascinated, and it was terribly well received. It transferred lock, stock and barrel down to New York, where it went remarkably well again and finally we brought it over here in trepidation. And although by this time I don't think it was such a good production — it had gone a bit stale with my having done it three times — it had a terribly good press. I thought we'd have been hit over the head for such a wicked play and then, out of the blue, the libel action started and it obliged us to take the play off. It eventually cost a lot of money; it was one of those unfortunate things, there was one person alive who was mentioned in the play. It was a very exciting and very alarming experience.'

And *Oh! Calcutta!* Once it was described as absolutely filthy, then everyone was bound to go. 'I suppose so. But we

didn't think so at the time. I'd seen it in America, and I
thought it was awful. I hated it. No, I didn't exactly hate it,
I just loathed it. It was so poor. I had great visions of making
it better here, and in some areas it is, though not entirely. We
weren't at all certain that it would go well here, and indeed
in one sense it was touch and go because after the Roundhouse
season — where it did frightfully well — we couldn't get a
theatre and we were desperate, thinking in terms of tents and
old barns, anything. Shaftesbury Avenue wouldn't touch it.
The Royalty, where it went, seemed entirely wrong, too
large and so on, but in the event it proved to be a very good
theatre as it was very large and was soon full.

'We really didn't think it would get the sort of reaction it
got here. We never thought in terms of a long run — we only
thought in terms of surviving legalistically. Would we be
allowed to open, would we be closed? Fortunately, the
Solicitor-General, very late in the day, said that he wouldn't
entertain private prosecution, so we were through — just.
No, I didn't think of it as a jokey production — anything
but. I didn't think of it as a light piece, I took it very
seriously and still do. Having said that, I mean I took a very
sententious attitude towards it and retain that attitude,
though I see perfectly clearly that it is not a heavyweight
evening at all, and perhaps I need to justify what I did. Also
because of the genuine sense that there was a necessity for
pushing the theatre into different avenues and through
different barriers. I saw it the other night for about the first
time in two years, and I was enormously pleased with it.

'No, I don't find any difference in the way I approach a
play for the commercial theatre and how I work with the
National or the RSC. How do I get down to it? By refusing
to — like most overworked people, I put off the evil hour.
I have an initial spasm of reading the play like a billy goat
four or five times, hopefully some time before I do it, then
I put it aside and do something else. Then I realize with
horror we're going into rehearsal the next day. I'm lucky
that during the last twelve years I've worked mainly with
two designers, Ralph Koltai and Abdul Farrah, and I've
taken them with me into these rather strange other things.
Abdul is an exclusively RSC designer, but he did *Calcutta*

with me. When Ralph did *Soldiers* he was almost entirely a
classical play and opera designer. They're both people I
enjoy working with on the decor right from the model, and
that's where I learn most about the play — in those long
discussions about the setting of the piece.

'I don't just like working with actors I know, I like working
with new people. One of the pleasures of the commercial
theatre is that you do extend your range of acquaintances,
which is marvellous. Even going back to the RSC isn't the
same. When I went back to do the *Shrew* I'd hardly worked
with any of those people. There are few people you work
with you don't know anything about, you've seem them in
other plays on the box and so on, so you have something to
go on. For instance, I asked Peter Egan to be in *What Every
Woman Knows,* I'd seen him in *Journey's End* and thought
he was fantastic in that and we duly worked together.
Dorothy Tutin, in the same play, I'd seen work at Stratford
but had never worked with her, while Gordon Jackson I'd
only seen in *Upstairs, Downstairs.* It was a good production,
that, with a splendid cast, but it never came into town
because we just couldn't get a theatre.

'I find working with American actors difficult and am less
able to judge their performances even though it's the same
language. I know it's even more difficult to understand
actors if, say, they only speak Serbo-Croat, but then you
expect it to be. You don't expect it to be as difficult as it is
when they speak the same language. I just don't know how
to 'read' them. Perhaps I haven't worked there enough. I do
find myself in America working in a more controlled way
than I do in England. I mean, I'm more careful what
questions I ask an actor, what suggestions I make, because
just as I don't fully understand them I suspect they don't
fully understand me in the way an English actor would. If I
stand on my head and start screaming swear-words at an
English actor he would know what Clifford means, but an
American would just think that I was angry with him. I
think the words one uses like realism, naturalism or style
tend to mean different things.

'Although I'm naturally interested in movement in plays
I'm also interested in the verbal aspect of theatre. The plays

I've always gone for when I've been going through a lot of
work in rep are plays by Beckett, Pinter, Rudkin, Ionesco,
verbal, poetic talents, I've always been interested too in
polemical theatre like Hochhuth, where what is said is
important, not the way it sounds. Both my *Twelfth Night*
and *Merchant of Venice* at Stratford were criticized for not
going deep enough into the poetry, though I know the
ground rules — you can't be at Stratford near John Barton
for twelve years and not know what the ground rules are.
Then in *Comedy of Errors* I was praised because the actors
spoke it very well, they did it very, very correctly. I had the
same reaction then to the *Shrew* as I did to *Twelfth Night*
where a great deal of the critical comment was along the
lines that there was too much movement and it was under-
spoken, so I'm beginning to wonder (though I'm constantly
in rehearsal on about text, text, text) that maybe I haven't
got the grip of it that I should have. Then again, the all-male
*As You Like It* was praised, and everyone said how well
spoken that was.

'It's so much, too, a question of the attitude of the cast
when you go into rehearsal. I remember clearly the *As You
Like It* at the National, where most of the cast hadn't done
a new play for over a month and were actually raring to go.
At Stratford that doesn't always happen. They're in rehearsal
from January until the last play opens. So it's not a question
of how many weeks you've got but how many hours, and
with actors in what kind of state. It's so different in Europe,
where they work only four hours of rehearsal a day, and then
open when they're ready. They don't dig you asking when
you arrive what day the play will open, because you have
other things to do, they just tell you to work at it. What
they're trying to avoid is this terrible English habit of the
fixed opening night. They don't have that awful ten to one, two
to five thirty and then an evening performance which is the lot
of the English repertory actor.

'Still, as things are I can't see the system here changing
much, so if I want to work in it then I just have to accept it.
I suppose it's only when I talk like this, I realize I've done
quite a lot of work. Most of the time I feel I haven't really
done much, I've just been messing around.'